Praise for *Inequality by Design*

"The timing of this book could not be more critical as current events and policies of the past increase economic divides in America. Mattson and Johnson have brought clarity to the financial shifts our nation has experienced, calling us to pay attention.

The authors start by painting a grim picture, but there is hope. They cast a vision for meaningful impact within this generation as well as generations to come. They acknowledge the anecdotal stories that influence us, but they never lose sight of the significance of the community-level data that paints the full picture in which we all live. The text is conversational, making it approachable no matter your expertise in economics, social structures, or policy. This is a must read for anyone hoping to influence healing in America. As Mattson and Johnson conclude, 'We truly are all in this together.'"

— **Robin E. Johnson, MD, MPH,** *Emergency Medicine, Public Health, Community Advocate and Educator*

"Mattson and Johnson paint a very clear picture of the economic, political, and social crossroads that we find ourselves in today, weaving history, economics, and storytelling together to make an approachable and informative glimpse of our American times. Local and civic leaders should take heart in their "paths for people" and "paths for policy," which provide concrete ways we can address the growing inequality in our system before it reaches a point of no return."

— **Mike Rasmussen, MA***, Community Leader and Small Business Owner*

Inequality by Design

How a Rigged Economy Fractures America and What We Can Do About It

Ryan Mattson and Ben Johnson

Inequality by Design: How a Rigged Economy Fractures America and What We Can Do About It

Copyright © 2025 by Ryan Mattson and Ben Johnson

Published by Upriver Press
P.O. Box 51455
Colorado Springs, CO 80949
upriverpress.com

ISBN Print Version: 9798990623644
ISBN Ebook: 9798990623651

Library of Congress Control Number: 2025933948

Cover Design: James Clarke (jclarke.net)

Printed in the United States of America

Upriver Press publishes books by leading scholars and industry experts who bring well-researched, evidence-based ideas to public discourse. The views of our authors do not necessarily represent the opinions of the staff at Upriver Press.

Inequality by Design

How a Rigged Economy Fractures America and What We Can Do About It

Ryan Mattson and Ben Johnson

upriver
PRESS

Contents

Contents

CHAPTER 1

A Tale of Three High School Graduates

Early Morning, May 1980

In a small midwestern city, three young adults wake up to their alarm clocks. The big day is here; today they graduate from high school. They occasionally attend the same classes, but on the weekends, they hang out with different circles of friends. They will not sit near each other during today's ceremony, and after the ceremony, they will return home to different parts of town. Like many others across America, these young people are about to take their first tentative steps into adulthood. Today, after throwing their caps in the air, they will embark on quite different paths.

All three hesitantly believe their teachers' promises: If they work hard and behave, they will have a shot at making it in the adult world. What the teachers do not tell them is that vast, impersonal forces will shape their lives. These forces will originate neither from God nor nature but instead in corporate boardrooms, and in the minds of pliant legislators and presidents. The economic changes set in motion in the years after their graduation day will define their lives, the lives of their children, and even their grandchildren.

Jenny silences her alarm clock and gets out of bed before

anyone else in her two-bedroom house. Her younger sister tells her to go back to sleep, but Jenny wants to prepare for graduation. Her mom takes her to the beauty store for last-minute cosmetics and then to the hairdresser, an outing that requires Jenny's younger sister to finally wake up and look after their little brother.

During the whole morning, Jenny thinks about starting a life with her high school sweetheart. These dreams distract her from the tasks at hand. Like many young people on the verge of adulthood, she is naive and overly confident. That is not a bad thing because she will need confidence, self-assurance, and the willpower to overcome the obstacles between reality and her aspirations: fame, fortune, and a piece of the American dream somewhere in sunny California.

Our next high school grad, Marty, wakes up in a bad mood. Nothing went right during the last semester. Due to his poor spelling and lack of attention to sentence structure, he must take a remedial summer course with an English teacher who already failed him twice. Marty will walk the stage, but getting his diploma will depend on whether he can pass summer school. What neither Marty nor the teacher know is that Marty lives with undiagnosed dyslexia.

Marty mopes about the apartment. His mom is already working the breakfast counter. His stepdad, who is trying to sleep after working the night shift, implores him to turn down the radio. Marty expects this from his stepdad, but even his little brother Bruce gets on his case. Their protests force Marty to leave, to find some friends with whom to spend the morning.

Then there is Chad. Born into a wealthy family, Chad wakes up in his own private bedroom. He takes a long morning shower (his family's utilities have never been shut off by the gas company). He does not worry that his father's paycheck might be spent before food lands on the table, but his life is not all sunshine and rainbows. After all, he recently broke up with his senior-year girlfriend because she did not want to leave town when he went to college. And just yesterday he got a rejection letter from his first-choice university. Chad eats a filling breakfast and hops on his motorcycle, riding from one friend's house to another, checking in to find out which of them had received a college acceptance letter and scholarship award.

At the graduation ceremony, Jenny, Marty, and Chad walk the stage wearing the same traditional garb. Jenny carries a bouquet she received from her boyfriend. Marty trips on the last step to the stage, physically stumbling through the end of high school. Chad's back pocket holds a letter confirming his acceptance to a prestigious East Coast university; not his first choice, but not a bad option. After posing for pictures with family, friends, and teachers, the auditorium doors close. Only the janitor stays late, cleaning up confetti and programs.

Lunchtime, June 1990

The noonday sun shines down on Reagan's America. The political baton has passed to George H.W. Bush and people believe the coming decade holds great promise. Communism is in retreat. The reforms of the previous ten years have pushed down taxes, slashed regulations, and gutted unions. Although trumpeted in the media as game-changing improvements, the reforms have begun to undermine the working and middles classes. Main Street in our trio's hometown features whitewashed windows and vacant stores. Factories and mills stand empty. The nation's financial institutions are still shaky after the 1987 stock market crash and the Savings and Loan crisis.

Broader economic trends *seem* far removed from Jenny, Marty, and Chad—all three are caught up in the dynamism of life in their late twenties—but the policies of the previous decade affect their lives in ways both obvious and subtle.

Jenny is a proud but constantly harried mother of two. Her boyfriend never bought her that ring. In fact, the boyfriend disappeared, leaving only a note saying he would send money when he could. Her oldest, Luke, turns eight this year. His teachers compliment Jenny on her son's easy mastery of multiplication and division. Critical of her own choices, Jenny quietly credits the school more than her own efforts for Luke's success. His little sister, Ruby, who will start kindergarten in the fall, desperately wants a real hamster for her birthday. She will have to settle for a stuffed hamster.

Fortunately, Jenny's meager wages still cover the basics for her and the kids. Thanks to a Section 8 housing voucher program, Jenny rents an apartment at below-market rates. The apartment is not nice, but it provides enough stability to keep the kids in the same school district. When she gets a moment to herself, she does not think about the legislative wrangling that will soon ratchet up the cost for voucher recipients like her. She only knows what the lady at the HUD office told her: If her wages exceed the federal poverty line, she will no longer qualify for the program. In a perverse way, she and her kids are slightly better off being poor. For now.

A few years after graduation, Marty's new girlfriend persuades him to earn a GED. Wanting to impress her, Marty finds a remedial English class at the local community college. The course is affordable, even on a material handler's wages. The instructor recommends testing, which leads to a diagnosis of dyslexia. Again, thanks to the ample government investment in post-secondary education, Marty can afford a second course that teaches techniques for living with his condition. This help, which he never received as a kid, opens the world of written knowledge in a way he had never experienced. Encouraged by his academic progress, Marty earns a journeyman welder's license.

Now Marty *works*. He accepts all the overtime, all the extra shifts, and all the weekends he can get. With the unending layoffs, the defeat of a unionization vote at the factory, and the state legislation that allows at-will firing, he cannot say no to a shift. Rumors that the factory has been sold fly around the shop floor. His fellow workers have heard that the sale has nothing to do with selective layoffs or "downsizing"; rather, the company is sending machines overseas. Marty considers rage-quitting until a buddy points out that it will be difficult for the company to account for small tools during the move. The two men had previously talked about starting their own business and now they see an opportunity. They knew that small business loans were hard to come by, but unattended hand tools were not.

Chad is now a graduate of his well-heeled East Coast university, where each summer he enjoyed a white-collar internship. The last one led to an entry-level position in the acquisitions office of a large commercial bank. Like Marty, Chad has been working long hours, but unlike Marty, he is not worried about getting fired. He stays in the office because he hopes to secure a promotion. Today is the day. Chad's boss tells him he has been selected for a supervisory role and that he will have at least four fresh-faced grads working directly under him.

As a little reward to himself, Chad spontaneously decides to fly home, first class, to attend his ten-year class reunion. As the plane lands, Chad looks forward to sitting on a patio and raising a glass with friends he has not seen in five years. At the reunion, he notices that his senior-year ex has put on a lot of weight. He does not notice the absence of Jenny or Marty. Chad had known them a little in high school, but at that time Jenny had a steady boyfriend and Marty was usually hanging out with pot-smoking kids behind the prefabs. At least that was the rumor.

Afternoon, August 2000

The summer of 2000 is not the hottest on record; that ignominious title belonged to the summer of 1998. But it is hot. The dotcom bubble has burst, at least if the numbers on the Nasdaq Index mean anything. The political conventions of the two major parties wrap up amid tepid public enthusiasm for electing one of two Baby Boomers from a southern state. Why should they be enthusiastic? After all, the previous decade had produced the triumph of neoliberal economic policies across the political spectrum and around the globe, so why get excited about electoral politics?

Most Americans do not notice or care about the recent repeal of the Depression-era Glass-Stegall Act, even though by removing this legal barrier between commercial and investment banking, Congress exposed the commercial and home-lending markets to the boom-bust cycles of betting and speculation—inherent to Wall Street. As automation pumps up corporate profits, the jobs of millions of American workers are becoming redundant. The working class is losing ground, but at least the cost of consumer goods keeps dropping. Those in power repeatedly promise that a rising tide will lift all boats, eventually.

Jenny has moved back home from California to be close to family. Repeated budget cuts have driven down the value of her housing vouchers while driving up the share of her income required to pay rent. Jenny and her kids live with a mostly employed boyfriend in a trailer park on the "wrong side of the tracks." This means the wrong side of a noisy highway, which makes it hard to sleep. As it was in California, Jenny finds the social safety net fraying in the Midwest. "Welfare reforms" in the mid-1990s have disqualified her from receiving government assistance, adding to the instability in her life.

During his constant moves from one school district to another, Luke, her formerly wide-eyed son, fell in with the wrong crowd. He turns eighteen this year, a milestone that will wipe clean his juvenile legal record. Now he talks about joining the military to get out of his circumstances. She keeps her thoughts to herself, but Jenny also wants a change in circumstances: relief from the sweltering heat that permeates the trailer, and relief from the relationship with a man whose name is on the trailer's lease. Her daughter, Ruby, is starting to date boys, but Jenny can barely get time to talk to her about choosing the "right" guy. She works as many shifts as she can at the restaurant and temps as a janitor. Her paychecks do not go as far as they used to; the gap between average wage earners and low-paid workers like her continues to grow.

Marty's welding company had kept him financially afloat over the previous decade, but now profits have been declining.

The girlfriend-turned-wife who had encouraged him to get a GED recently pressed him to look for a more stable job. Because she was right about the GED, Marty starts sending out resumes. In the cover letter, he argues that running his own business should qualify him for a middle management position. Fortunately, the hiring manager for a big box store agreed. He, his wife, and their three kids—all born between 1992 and 1999—make the move from a dying post-industrial city to a bustling suburb outside Chicago.

Stable employment allows Marty and spouse to breathe a little easier. With middle age setting in, they enjoy watching their kids grow up. The kids are expensive, but his mom has moved in to help with childcare and the big box store has decent, albeit increasingly expensive, health insurance for when they get runny noses. Marty grumbles about property taxes, but buying a house at the edge of the good school district gives his kids learning opportunities that his hometown school district can no longer afford to offer.

The dotcom bust is a headache for Chad. His job and personal wealth are not at risk, but the portfolios he manages show declining returns. While waiting for his BMW's air conditioning to cool the soupy, stifling air, Chad listens to a radio story about the repeal of Glass-Stegall. An adage he learned from an early mentor runs through his head; always trust finance to make money when manufacturing or tech sectors falter.

He breathes a sigh of relief. With the old regulation gone, he can now move into the riskier technology bets. Chad knows he must be a shark, operating with bold instincts, to succeed in finance. He begins to wonder if now is a good time to move from wealth management to wealth creation. (Chad knows people in the investment banking community who might hire him.) If not, he figures he can start his own investment bank. He ponders ideas about where to loan cheap money obtained from the Federal Reserve's banking window.

His thoughts shift from high-finance schemes to personal matters; specifically, how to spend the upcoming long weekend. Throw a party at his large house in Connecticut? Fly west to his condo in Aspen for some fresh mountain air? Spend time in Miami with his twenty-one-year-old girlfriend? After glancing at the printed invitation to his twenty-year high school reunion, he quickly excludes that option. Why go back to the square-state town where he grew up to chat with people he barely remembers?

Evening, November 2010

The 2008 Global Financial Crisis, which was almost as devastating as the 1929 Great Depression, happened about two years earlier. The crash's dire effects are now becoming clear. Official unemployment is around 10 percent, though by many measures it runs higher. Six million families have been evicted from their homes. On the face of it, the 4.3 percent drop in GDP during this recession does not sound that bad, but news reports say it is the largest contraction of the US economy since the end of World War II. With Barack Obama in the White House, American military involvement in Iraq is slowly ending.

How long the US will stay out of the Middle East remains to be seen. The question haunts Jenny, whose son, Luke, is in the middle of his third overseas tour with the Air Force, this time in Afghanistan. He sends a decent amount of money home each month to help Jenny with rent, but he is ready to leave the military and try civilian life. Jenny looks forward to her son's safe return, but she worries that a stateside job will not pay well enough for Luke to help the family.

And they need help. Jenny lost both her jobs during the 2008 crash. Now she alternates between working mornings at a downtown parking lot booth and evenings at janitorial jobs through a temp agency. Not yet fifty, she can already feel arthritis creeping into her hands with every wastebasket she empties and every push of the mop bucket.

She shares a one-room apartment with her daughter, Ruby, and her newborn granddaughter, Allison. Ruby recently lost her job as a filing clerk at a local hospital. She has applied for a job at a health insurance company, which will soon benefit from federal subsidies passed in the Affordable Care Act. Ruby hears stories about hiring managers who exclude candidates with low credit scores. Due to the last eviction, her score is less than optimal. Homelessness is one missed rent check away.

Marty is also deeply worried. The big box store where he had been working closed due to the recession. His wife still works as a guidance counselor, but she earns half what Marty did. Now, due to his job loss, the family faces a lack of health insurance. Marty's savings should cover routine visits to the doctor, but an emergency could wipe them out financially. Between emailing resumes, Marty is tormented by doubts about how to afford his son's education.

Marty Jr. has worked hard at school and hopes to get a bachelor's degree in computer science at the state's flagship university, a degree that should pay good returns. But Marty also thinks about his middle child, Jillian, who is wrapping up her first year of high school, and his youngest, Bobby, who is starting middle school in the fall. All the kids express a desire to go to college, but Marty knows the family cannot afford tuition for three. Moreover, his borderline diabetes has become harder to regulate with diet and exercise, and now that he lacks health insurance, he is fearful that he will not be able to afford medication—if needed—without a new job. And who wants to hire a man in his late forties to manage a retail store?

Chad lost a boatload of money in the wake of the financial crisis, but he worries more that Congress will allow the Bush tax cuts of 2001-2002 to expire. If that happens, Chad expects his federal tax rate to reach 15 percent. He knows that is far lower than what less-wealthy Americans pay, but the possibility is upsetting. Socially liberal, he likes Obama's calm demeanor, but he cannot stomach paying higher taxes.

Sitting at the dinner table with a mail-order wife half his age, Chad turns up the TV to watch midterm election coverage. Recent Supreme Court rulings and the potential sunsetting of Bush tax cuts have inspired Chad to join lobbying efforts with other multimillionaires—to support anti-tax candidates. His wife interrupts his thoughts, asking if he intends to take them to the beach for Christmas or to his hometown. Chad grumbles that he should move his parents to a closer retirement home—so that he never has to go back to that place.

Midnight, December 2020

Big headlines fill TV screens: terror attacks abroad, political instability at home, and a global pandemic that rivals the 1918-1921 Spanish Flu. Modern medical care keeps the death rate in the developed world lower than a century before, but the long-term effects of a Covid-19 infection remain unclear. Many Americans doubt the severity of the disease. The pandemic triggers another major financial shock, sending the official unemployment rate to 13 percent and shrinking the country's GDP by 1 percent. Hidden in the economic data are harsh trends which, if they receive media attention, elicit no substantive policy response from Washington or corporate board rooms. Hourly wages stagnate. House prices continue to rise. Debts from student loans, home loans, and credit cards continue to pile up as purchasing power sinks.

Shivering in her car, Jenny drives south to avoid the next wave of wintry weather. In the back seat, wedged between suitcases and a duffle bag, Ruby and Allison sleep. Both adults in the car have lost their jobs—along with millions of other service workers since the start of the pandemic.

As she drives, tears fill Jenny's eyes. Her son, Luke, made it home from Afghanistan, but he could not shake the psychological damage that came from years on the front lines of the "war on terror." Minor injuries on a construction site combined with PTSD and easy access to pain pills drove him into a sickening sobriety-to-relapse cycle. Despite her motherly efforts, Luke died in the fall of 2019. He was one of sixty-two thousand Americans to die of a drug overdose that year, more than all the soldiers who died in US wars since 1945.

Moving to a warmer climate, she hopes, will ease her arthritis pain and provide a fresh start for the surviving family. Grim resolve motivates her during the drive south in her 1990 Toyota. She no longer has the giddy optimism that she had while driving to California forty years earlier.

Marty's wife and kids sit glumly at home, watching Christmas lights blink on the tree. They are chilled to the bone after standing in biting wind at the graveside service. The previous year or so, while working long hours as a burger joint manager, Marty had found little time to keep up with his diet, exercise routine, or visits to doctors. His work schedule had proved deadlier than stagnant wages and soaring medical costs. Marty's diabetes had swung wildly as the family struggled to pay for insulin. He did not die of Covid-19, at least not directly. As hospital ICUs overflowed with sick people, Marty had clung to life in the emergency room for two days while high blood sugar ravaged his body. The damage had compounded, quickly leading to multisystem organ failure. Dead at fifty-eight. As the Christmas lights flicker, a lawyer reads his will. There is not much to split between the grieving spouse and children. They would all rather have Marty back home alive.

Chad, despite making and losing a lot of money during the previous decade, still finds himself just below the top 1 percent of wealthiest Americans. Getting into that club requires enormous amounts of personal capital, which Chad simply does not have. But he has no real financial worries. He has the freedom to think about partisan politics morning to night. He is thrilled with the outcome of the 2020 elections; the candidates to whom he and his wealthy friends had generously contributed had triumphed.

This new experience of engaging in politics—to use his money to shape economic and tax policy—feels invigorating and dynamic. Chad enjoys the camaraderie of friends who all invest money to weave a system of laws and tax codes designed to overwhelmingly benefit his class. Despite his wealth, he is eager to leverage what he has for further gains and more political influence. No matter the size of the pond, he reasons, there is always a bigger fish.

Turning off the TV, Chad leaves his house for a flight to Miami with his new mail-order wife. He keeps his fingers crossed that the incoming cold front will not ground private jets. As the plane takes off, Chad notices that one of his investment ventures involves relocating an assembly plant from a small Midwestern city to Mexico. Only belatedly does he realize it is the city he grew up in. He mutters that the workers who will soon lose their jobs should have learned to code.

CHAPTER 2

Measuring Our Economic Malaise

Are these fictitious individuals anomalies? We do not think so. As the economic stratification of American society has accelerated over the last forty or more years, the lives of millions of people like Marty and Jenny have been upended and cut short, all in the interest of maximizing the profits of those at the top. The Chads of the world have always had incentives to join the elite club, so those near the top remain loyal to the system even if it means ignoring the increasingly dire plight of those below them.

The decades described in the previous chapter have resulted in stratospheric levels of inequality. It is not the first time in US history that this has occurred, but if the past serves as a guide to the future, current conditions will push Americans to make desperate, dangerous choices. More on that later.

We first need to look at the economic trends that led to our current situation. Over the course of our three protagonists' lives, huge sums of wealth and the economic clout that comes with it, flowed ever upward to the wealthiest Americans. For Jenny, the purchasing power of her already low-paying jobs only eroded over time. The year she graduated from high school, the gap between the federal minimum wage and the average wage was about $10 per hour (in 2023 dollars). Today, that gap is $21 per hour. This means that the poor became increasingly poorer than average wage earners.

The downward trend has also negatively affected most middle-class Americans. The wage gap has weakened the purchasing power of *anyone* whose hourly wages total less than $57,000 per year. In raw numbers, this wage gap affects at least 40 percent of the US workforce, about sixty-seven million workers (based on 2019 data). Figure 2-1 below shows how the gap between real wages and the federal minimum wage has widened since 1964. (As the line rises, the gap increases.)

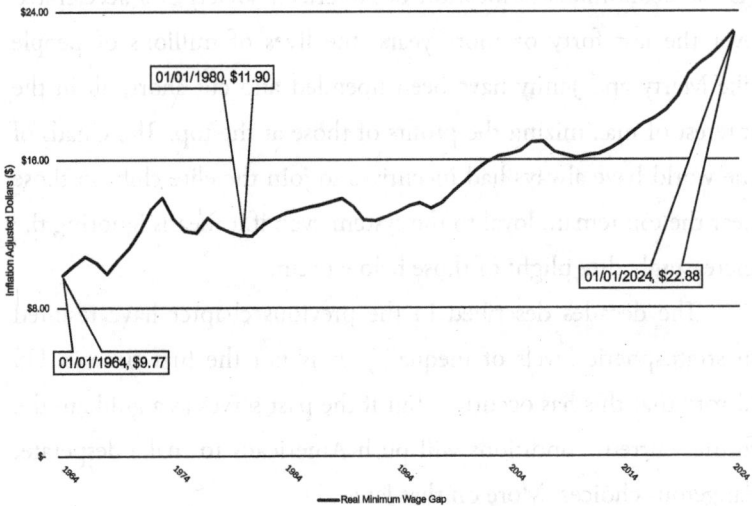

Figure 2-1: Changes in the US real wage gap between the federal minimum wage and average wages. Source: US Department of Labor, the Bureau of Labor Statistics, and author calculations

The erosion of wages has not only affected those who earn hourly pay. Even if a person draws a salary, he or she should consider the relationship between income and purchasing power. We can evaluate purchasing power by using measures like "GDP per capita."

As a reminder, GDP (gross domestic product) measures the amount of money spent on goods and services within an economy. Thus, GDP "per capita" represents the amount of money each person would need to spend to afford an "average" amount of goods and services. This number, GDP per capita, does not represent the amount each person earns; rather, it shows the average share of economic activity per person.

Terms like *GDP* and *per capita* can seem abstract, so it helps to engage in a thought experiment. Imagine that ten people live in a simple economy that produces $1000 in goods and services. The GDP would be $1000. Divided evenly, the per-capita GDP would be $100 dollars for each of the ten people. Because GDP measures consumption, the per-capita number really means that each of the ten people in this fictional economy would need $100 of income each year to buy the average amount of goods and services. Or we can say that each person can "fully participate" in the economy if he or she earns $100 of income per year. Thus, GDP per capita represents a benchmark of spending necessary for all participants in an economy to engage with each other in efficient and productive ways.

If we drop Jenny, Marty, and Chad into this fictional $1000-per-year economy, the ideal would be for each of them to make $100 and spend $100 each year. This would be the perfect "GDP per person" scenario. Income equals expenditure, which is equally divided across the population.

However, the ideal economy described above does not reflect reality. As stated earlier, a gap began to grow in the 1980s between per-capita GDP and income. If we use the fictional economy to illustrate the real economy, Jenny would make $60 and consume

23

$70 a year. She would have to make up the difference by borrowing from or bartering with family, friends, and neighbors. Marty would earn $80 and consume $60, which would allow him to save for a rainy day. Chad would make $160 and spend $170 per year.

Notice that for Jenny to engage fully in the economy, she would have to *overspend* significantly. By contrast, Chad makes far more than the average, but he also spends much more than the $100 needed to fully participate in the economy. Those time-share condos and second houses are not cheap. Chad expects to make more next year, so he believes he can afford to overspend.

In today's real economy, those who do not earn enough to fully participate in the economy become increasingly marginalized and left behind. It gets worse year after year. The following chart (figure 2-2) tracks the gap between the median income of a household and the per-worker GDP in the United states since 1967.

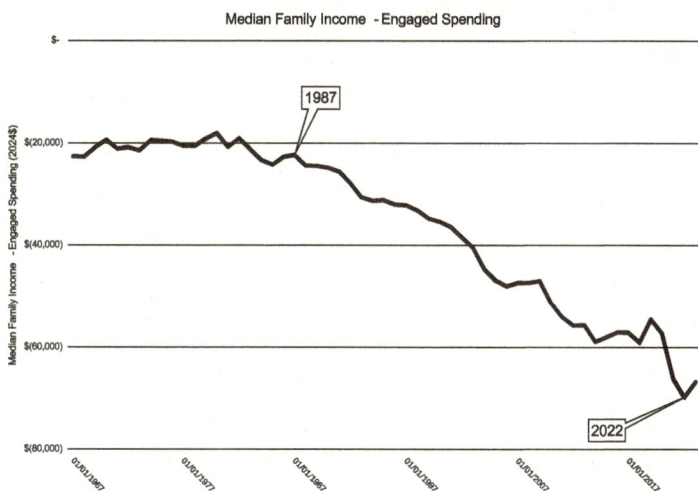

Figure 2-2: The difference in median family income and engaged economic spending (GDP per worker) dropped sharply throughout the 1980s. As this number grows increasingly negative, it shows that the median US family increasingly cannot afford to be "economically engaged" as measured by GDP. Source: US Census, the Bureau of Economic Analysis, and the authors' calculations

Figure 2-2 demonstrates that since the late 1960s, half of US households (median) were able to maintain engaged spending as national wealth increased. In other words, they were able to continue participating fully in the economy. American workers in the 1960s and 1970s were about $20,000 under the mark, but they were not $70,000 under the mark, as was the case in 2023. The situation began to worsen in about 1980. That is when the average American's share of national wealth began to fall precipitously. Fewer and fewer people since then have been able to fully participate in the US economy. Those who are falling behind find it harder to buy what they need to maintain an "average" lifestyle, as measured by GDP.

The graph above also demonstrates that we have been experiencing slow, generational economic changes in the US. Previous generations of Americans went through tough economic times, such as the recessions of the 1960s and 1970s, but during those decades, a person earning an average income could fully participate in the economy. Policy decisions from 1980 onward, which changed the rules of the game, dramatically worsened the economic situations of most Americans who entered the workforce in the late 1970s and early 1980s, and every year since.

It is important to remember that the gap between median household wages and the amount needed to participate fully in the economy *has been expanding*. Even when accounting for inflation, Americans must spend more of their stagnant wages to maintain an average lifestyle.

Today many people say they feel poorer, but they struggle to explain why. That is because the big economic headlines usually seem positive. The description above explains why most Americans experience increased financial hardship even when they work hard and even during times of robust growth in the overall economy. Today, if a woman makes $66,000 per year but she needs $81,000 to cover her basic annual household costs, she will experience economic malaise—even when the national GDP is growing and unemployment is low.

As stated above, this disparity started to grow in the 1980s. From that year forward, the US GDP continued to grow but more money flowed to the high-wealth sectors of the economy, such as computing, real estate, insurance, and finance. Because of Reagan-era policy changes, most of that money began flowing to an ever-smaller number of people. Under the new rules, most Americans began to fall behind. In contrast with previous generations, Americans after the 1970s saw their share of national wealth increasingly decline even as the national GDP increased. Most Americans have been "playing by the rules"—working hard, studying, paying taxes, being good citizens—but the rules have been rigged to work against them.

Jenny, Marty, and Chad graduated from high school in 1980, a time when the median household income was more than sufficient for full economic engagement (according to GDP). But as Jenny and Marty entered the workforce, and as they continued their careers and lives, this *surplus* of income dropped to $0 by 1990. After 1990, their levels of surplus income dropped even further each year into deficit territory. As Jenny and Marty progressed through the second half of adulthood, their buying power was eaten away by rising costs and stagnant wages, with no respite. The degree to which each household operates at a deficit represents another year of unpaid bills, payday loans, and credit card debt; that is, another year of not making ends meet.

Myths that Perpetuate Inequality

There are several myths about inequality in the US. As with any false notion of reality, these myths have perpetuated the problem and its underlying causes, making it "sticky" (hard to repair). False conceptions about our economic designs have allowed inequality to grow and persist since the 1970s. Thus, younger generations who grew up with the gradual expansion of wealth disparities often think that inequality is normal. Likewise wealthier people from older generations either think that younger generations are not working hard enough, or they think that inequality is "not a big deal" because it "does not affect me." This disinterest does not necessarily stem from a lack of empathy; rather, older generations simply do not perceive the grievous economic changes that younger generations have inherited.

Many of the trends we will discuss in the book have gone on for two or three generations. As the gap between the wealthy and everyone else has gradually widened, those of us outside the top 1 percent have simply adapted to getting a little poorer every year. To younger generations who have grown up in our current economy, the adaptations required of them seem like "common sense," even though nothing about the economic situation fits the definition of "common" or "sensical."

People whose incomes used to put them in the middle of the bell curve are now being pushed down the income ladder in real terms as their buying power declines. At the same time, the 1 percent and those who are almost able to join that group become demonstrably richer. We have reached a point at which the bell curve no longer helpfully illustrates the starkly different economic worlds in which American's find themselves.

There is a better visual representation of our situation today than the bell curve. Imagine instead the Liberty Bell, that iconic symbol of American independence that is on display in Philadelphia. Now imagine that the big crack in the bell spreads farther apart leading to a complete fragmentation. In economic terms, that is happening in the US. One small fragment is gaining more wealth while everyone else is less able to generate wealth in relation to the cost of living. Skipping lattes and avocado toast will not stop that trend.

Myth 1: Top-Line Economic Numbers Apply to Everyone

Most people form opinions about economic conditions by looking at top-line numbers like the GDP, stock market levels, per capita income, unemployment rates, or average annual wages. But those measures gloss over a messier situation. The spokespeople for the rich continually use them to say, "See! The situation isn't *that* bad. This inequality thing only affects the poor." That view is not true; inequality hurts *everyone*, except the wealthiest Americans.

Top-line economic indicators hide what is, for almost all Americans, a major financial struggle in daily life: the inability to save income and make investments. Consider a person who is living on $30,000 per year, or about $15 per hour and forty hours per week. This person would earn more than twice the federal minimum wage, but she would struggle to afford a basic life in most US cities. If she cares for a child or elderly person, or if she lives in a high-cost-of-living state, any financial cushion she might have will vanish. Still, at $30,000 a year, she might be able to squeeze a little blood from that stone. (Both of us, the authors, have been in that situation, and we suspect that most of our readers have too.) With luck and hard work, she might land a promotion or find a slightly higher paying job. But she will need to earn more to maintain her position relative to the US median income.

As discussed earlier in the chapter (see figure 2-1), the gap between the federal minimum wage ($15,000 per year) and the average US wage (roughly $56,000 a year) has more than doubled since 1980. In addition to the widening of this gap, more people are earning below-average incomes, people like our hypothetical $30,000 earner. Since 1980, the total number of Americans earning less than the national average has increased. So has the *percentage* of these people within the total workforce. From an historical perspective, this trend is relatively new. The Bureau of Labor Statistics shows that the gap between minimum and average wage earners remained steady until the early 1990s.

What does this worrisome trend mean? For starters, it means that many people—and not just the poor—are getting poorer. More Americans are experiencing a decline in purchasing power, *even if we exclude the effect of inflation.* This trend is bad enough for individuals, but it is also bad for society. As real wages decline, more people have less to spend on goods and services. They have less money to spend at the grocery store, less to spend on home maintenance, less to spend at local businesses, and less to spend on higher quality products. Lower real wages force more people to take out short-term loans, which often have long-term ruinous results for the borrowers. Meanwhile, due to the rules of the game (the policies and laws), wealth is inflating at the top of the income ladder.

Myth 2: Inequality Is "Normal" in a "Free" Market

Inequality has become ever more ingrained in the United States since 1980, so it has gradually come to be seen as "just the way things are." But there is nothing normal about today's economy. Inequality occurs, as the title of this book indicates, *by design.* The painful situations of most Americans are not the result of random fate. Americans are getting poorer because of high-level decisions that have played out horribly. It is not normal when many Americans, if they miss a single paycheck, will not be able to see a doctor. It is not normal when a hard-working man's unaffordable car repair turns his ride into a lawn ornament.

The normalization of inequality also leads to the common mantra that those who rise to the top should be praised for their hard work and that those who land at the bottom should be blamed for making bad choices. Regarding Chad, we might say, "Look how hard Chad is working! He's earned it!" About Marty, we might say, "He's working hard but not smart." To Jenny, some would say, "She should've thought twice before getting pregnant." No doubt some people choose self-destructive paths or make mistakes, but inequality in America is, at its root, a structural macroeconomic problem designed by politicians, policymakers, CEOs, and lobbyists.

The second half of the myth is that economic inequality is the byproduct of the "free market." Markets in the United States are not that free; instead, they are increasingly monopolistic. The consolidation of corporate power in every sector—food, banking, media, pharmaceuticals, and health care—pushes up the cost of basic survival. Consider, for example, how Amazon, Apple, Google, Meta, and other huge corporations affect so many aspects of our lives. Figure 2-3 below shows consolidation within the banking industry, which is just one example.

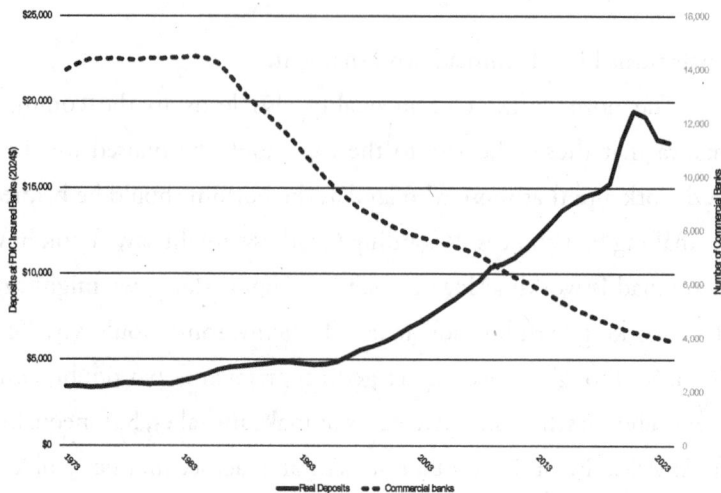

Figure 2-3: Monopolistic trends in the banking industry, with fewer banks managing more of Americans' money. Source: FDIC and the Board of Governors of the Federal Reserve System.

Despite the precipitous drop in the number of banks since the 1980s, the dollar value of deposits held by the remaining banks rose sharply in the 1990s. Today, fewer banks are holding more of our power to exchange, store, and invest.

According to Federal Reserve data, the concentration of the US banking system has increased the "spread" between the interest rates that banks charge for loans and what they pay to people who deposit money in savings accounts. By increasing the spread, banks improve their profit margins whereas average borrowers earn less on the money they save. This has occurred even when interest rates on loans reached record lows, such as after the Great Recession.

Any economist will tell you that the symptoms of concentrated market power (monopolistic trends) are higher prices, fewer suppliers, and less quantity on the market. The financial industry has been increasingly monopolistic, which worsens conditions for depositors, small firms, and anyone else who uses banking.

Within a context of market consolidation, the "competitive labor market" becomes increasingly monopsonistic. A *monopsony* occurs when the pool of employers is small due to monopolistic trends. In that situation, the small number of employers can force workers to accept lower wages. A monopsonistic economy lowers real wages in industries whose workers have no collective bargaining power. This problem is exacerbated at a macroeconomic level by a rigorous and disciplined monetary policy that tilts the scales in favor of what are now titan corporations with budgets larger than many countries.

In other words, even if a worker picks up all the overtime in the world, most profits from her labor will go to someone else. Because of macroeconomic policies, the money she brings home will lose value every year. Mortgage interest rates may drop, but the price of a house becomes attainable only to corporate buyers. Housing prices may drop, but the interest rates could rise to levels that make it impossible for potential home buyers to afford a loan. Either way, the corporate buyers win. Groceries become more expensive each month, wages never increase, and the Federal Reserve declares "victory over inflation." Due to the designs of our economy, which are now seen as normal, no amount of bootstrapping will be sufficient to grow the wealth of average Americans.

"Over the past decade, incomes among the middle class, the largest group in advanced countries, have stagnated or declined," writes Dr. Marion Laboure, a senior economist at Deutsche Bank and a lecturer at Harvard. "*Long-term structural trends* have played a considerable role in driving inequalities." (italics added).[1]

From about 1975 to 2018, average income growth did not occur even though the American GDP boomed. This wage stagnation occurred in stark contrast with what occurred between 1945 to 1975, a period in which income growth mirrored GDP growth. Figure 2-4 below, which displays what is often called the "great decoupling," provides a view of the historical situation. The upper line represents GDP growth and the lower line represents real average wages.

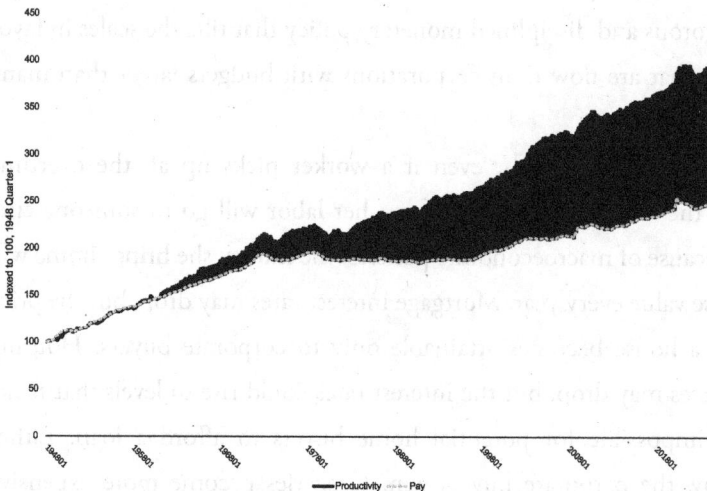

Figure 2-4: The "great decoupling" shows the widening gap between GDP (the upper edge of the gap) and average real wages (the lower edge of the gap), especially since the 1980s. Source: Economic Policy Institute[2]

What this means is that people who comprised the Greatest Generation, the Silent Generation, and the Baby Boomers saw average incomes increase in alignment with post-World War II economic GDP gains. That did not happen for more recent generations. For people coming of age in about 1980 and later, the American GDP continued to skyrocket, the wealthiest people took more of the nation's wealth, and average real incomes for most Americans stagnated. That dramatic negative outcome is not normal.

Consider the counterfactual. What might have happened if the 1945-1975 experience of older generations had continued; that is, what if the "great decoupling" had been the "great alignment"? What if incomes had increased in lockstep with the rise of GDP? For those within the median annual wage bracket, incomes would have risen to $92,000 (!) in 2018 rather than the actual amount of $50,000. (More on this below.) This is what the hollowing out of the middle-class does to people.

So Where Did the Money Go?

The growing disparity between national economic growth and average incomes leads to the next question; "Where's the money, Lebowski?" At least one answer comes from an unlikely place: the RAND Corporation, which is not exactly a bastion of left-wing Marxists. According to their 2020 study on "Trends in Income from 1975 to 2018," they found that over the last forty years nearly $50 trillion flowed from the bottom 99 percent of the American population to the top 1 percent.[3] That is an unfathomable amount of money. A billion dollars here, a billion dollars there, year after year, decade after decade. Even the fortune of a multimillionaire like our fictitious friend Chad would barely count as a rounding error.

It is difficult to comprehend $50 trillion. So, it might help to picture what a thousand bucks looks like, say ten $100 bills with that wise sage Benjamin Franklin on the front. Think about how you might like to spend a thousand bucks. With that in mind, remember that *every year* about $3500 worth of Benjamins that could have ended up in *your* pocket was snapped up by an exceedingly small group of wealthy people.

Now imagine what you might do with a million dollars. Would you pay off debts, perhaps those of family members or friends? Maybe make a few prudent investments? Take the family to Disney World for a week or two? Perhaps you would start a business, start a charity, or, saints preserve us, run for political office.

There is evidence that the $50 trillion reported by RAND *undercounts* the actual amount of wealth that has been redistributed upward in recent decades to the top 1 percent. The same RAND study concluded that if the wealth transfer had not happened, a counterfactual, then the average income *for the bottom fifth* of Americans would have been $61,000 rather than the actual $33,000.

If we could divide that $50 trillion among the approximately 330 million Americans alive today, each person would receive $151,515. However, because much of that wealth was bound up in stocks, bonds, and other assets, it would be more accurate in accounting terms to provide an annual figure. So, over the course of any given year during the past four decades, $1.25 trillion flowed to the balance sheets of the richest 1 percent. To calculate the per-person share of that $1.25 trillion, we should start with the US population in 1980, which was 226 million people. Likewise, we should remember that not everyone alive today has been alive since 1980. We also need to account for inflation. Taking all those factors into consideration, we can conclude that each American in the lower 99 percent saw the rough equivalent of $3,700 per year (1975 to 2018) move from their balance sheets to the top 1 percent (the richest three million people in the US).

This massive wealth transfer took a number of forms: corporate profits paid to shareholders rather than to the employees who created the profits; tax loopholes favoring capital gains over wages and salaries; monetary policy that functioned, as Mark Cuban said, as universal basic income for rich people; inflated rent and home prices which annually siphons earnings from workers to bankers and land speculators; and the dual impacts of rising education costs coupled with diminishing returns for that same education. These are a few of the "rules" that rig the economy in favor of the wealthy and design inequality for everyone else.

In this book, we will describe—in plain language—the impact of these factors on today's disconcerting situation. We believe it is important for everyone to understand the economic and policy forces that have been driving America's inequality. So much is at stake. History reminds us that horrible disasters have ruined highly unequal societies in the past. We would do well to remember that history and find ways to change direction before it is too late.

In each of the next chapters, we will discuss ways that we—individually and collectively—can hopefully stop the siphoning of wealth from the have-nots to those who have more than enough. The story will take you to some dark places, but in the end, we cast a positive vision for the future. Who does not like a happy ending?

Even that positive vision comes with a caveat. Jenny, Marty, and Chad *could* have had different lives if our political leaders over the past forty years had implemented policies aimed at allowing average Americans to keep more of the wealth they generate, as occurred in previous generations. When that wealth continually flows away from those who produce it, eventually there will be a reaction. If we do not overhaul our rigged economy, then what will happen in the decades to come?

Before we imagine the future, we first need to make our case—from an economics foundation—that inequality in America is not an imaginary condition. The numbers will leave little doubt in your mind that the situation is dire, and they will hopefully inspire you to act in positive ways to reverse this condition.

CHAPTER 3

Build your Wealth!
Buy a House!

Since we are writing about the current state of the American economy and the future of American society, an essential topic is the American house—that physical location with windows, doors, and walls where people gather to secure in the face of a chaotic and uncaring world. In the collective American imagination, owning a house symbolizes the achievement of economic and personal stability.

According to the Federal Reserve, the median sales price of a home in the first quarter of 2024 was $420,800. Home prices had been on an upward trend since the fourth quarter of 2011, when the average home sold for $259,000. The previous high sales price nationally, in the first quarter of 2007, was $322,000. These top-line numbers disguise the diversity of home prices. Real estate is a hyper-local market. For instance, in California a typical home in 2025 sold for about $800,000 while in states like Oklahoma and Kansas, houses sold for $202,000 and $222,000, respectively. Despite this diversity, the average sale price of a home is often greater than most people's 401k retirement funds.

A home can serve as a liquid asset, even without selling it. A person can borrow against the value of the house through a home equity line of credit (HELOC), or he can refinance the mortgage and pull equity if he needs quick cash. At a time when the real purchasing power for most Americans is in decline, owning a house takes on even greater financial and psychological importance.

Since 2020, some people have believed that the triple price shocks of the Covid-19 recession, the supply chain disruptions it created, and the inflation that followed had combined with stimulus checks to drive up home prices. However, between 50 to 60 percent of the rise in prices from 2021 to 2024 derived not from high labor costs or more expensive raw materials, but from profit taking. About half of the price increases in the early 2020s were driven by the desire of property owners and real estate investors to make more money while blaming inflation. Many markets in the United States bear more in common with markets captured by monopolies than markets that foster competition. The rise in home prices was *not* a result of more Americans having more cash to buy more homes. Those factors were not moving the supply and demand curves. That movement did not benefit most Americans. In this chapter, we will discuss restrictive zoning practices at the municipal level, the flood of speculative money, and the trend of real estate developers building for luxury units instead of starter homes.

None of this happens in a vacuum. Broader forces are pushing down housing supply even as demand rises. These factors include HOAs and the commodification of everything, as well as elite capture of local and state governments. But before we can launch into an examination of what has gone wrong in the housing market and the ways that individuals can overcome these trends, we need to talk about how a house relates to the nature of wealth.

How Much Is It Worth, Really?

Here is a straightforward question: "What is money?" A textbook definition is that money is anything that people agree to use as a store of value. People love using shiny metals like gold and silver for this purpose, but societies have also used everything from rocks to knotted rope. It does not really matter what the store of value is. What really matters is that the store of value represents *a claim on future goods or services.* In modern times, most Americans use their houses as one way to store long-term value. On average, Americans dedicate between 30 and 50 percent of their income to buying a house over the course of fifteen to thirty years, so it is fair to say that most Americans use a home, rather than a dollar, as a primary store of value.

This may seem pedantic and unnecessary to discuss, but it is worth taking a moment to think about the implications of using a house as a store of value. For instance, if a person has only paid half of a thirty year mortgage, does that mean her wealth equals the $420,000 average home price, or does it mean that her stored wealth in the house equals the principal that she has paid? Similarly, is it better to invest heavily in paying off a home mortgage and do so by reducing contributions to a 401(k)? In other words, is a home a better store of value for retirement than a retirement fund? These are complicated questions. The value of retirement funds, for example, is usually tied to fluctuating stock market returns. Or imagine if you had to choose between having a bank statement with the number $400,000 printed on it or four walls and a roof over your head. Which is a better store of value? Is shelter worth more than a future claim on goods and services?

A home can serve as both collateral and a place to stay warm in cold weather. A home keeps us healthy and secure. According to Maslow's Hierarchy of Needs, basics like food, clothing, shelter, and safety are top priorities in life. When those needs are met, the people can address higher-order issues like meaning and self-fulfillment. For this reason, people often overlook the psychological toll of feeling locked out of home ownership. That said, a house can be *both* a store of value and a source of wealth.

We need a more holistic understanding of housing's role in the future trajectory of America. After all, if Americans are denied access to shelter, then they will become increasingly frustrated with current economic designs. Indeed, tearing down the status quo that denies them basic shelter and safety becomes a "rational" action. And a lot of people are locked out of home ownership.

Americans since the late 1970s have experienced a dramatic tightening of the housing market. According to the Census Bureau, there were 126.8 million occupied housing units in the US in 2020. Of that total, 80.1 million units were occupied by the owner. This means that the overall home ownership rate is 63 percent.[4] This is the lowest home ownership rate since the 1979 census. The remaining 46.8 million units are renter-occupied. The total number of rental units increased by 14.8 percent from 2010 to 2020, outpacing the growth of owner-occupied units.[5] Of these rental units, 14.3 million (33 percent) were single-family houses, either detached or duplexes.[6] Additionally, the percentage of houses that were vacant but for sale fell from 2.4 percent in 2010 to 1.5 percent in 2020. This trend occurred as the rate of vacant *rentals* declined from 9.2 percent in 2010 to 7.4 percent in 2020. All this data indicates a tight housing market that favors the seller over the buyer.

Once again, we see a dramatic generational difference. Older generations benefited from easier access to home ownership compared to today's younger generations. The rate of home ownership for those under thirty-five declined from 45 percent in 1990 to 39 percent in 2020. This measure probably undercounts the decline in young-adult home owners. A study by the Urban Institute shows that the percentage of home owners under age thirty-five in 2020 was 29 percent, when we control for young adults who live with their parents or live with multiple roommates.[7] There is nothing wrong with multigenerational living or communal living, but one wonders how many of these arrangements are by choice.

In addition to the owned and rented units, the Census Bureau reports that there are 4.4 million vacant homes that are used for seasonal or recreational use. That number is more than twice the 1.9 million units that are vacant but for sale. In other words, there are more time-shares and beachfront condos than normal homes for average Americans.

Market Forces: Speculation, Investment, and Money Supply

This leads us to the first of many points about the dangers inherent in the way the economy rations housing. Real estate, especially homes, has become a form of speculation. Strange as it may sound, speculation is not necessarily bad. When speculation pays off, we tend to call that prudent investing. If someone put money into a company that fabricated computers in 1981, that speculation justified itself by yielding tremendous financial rewards. The flipside is that speculation does not always lead to riches. Usually, it leads to a crash or even destitution. We need only look back to the subprime housing crisis of 2007 through 2009 to see the result of speculation gone wrong. It was not an accident that the worst financial crisis since the 1929 stock market arose in the housing market.

It is important to make a distinction between money, assets, and wealth. Money or assets can also be used to speculate (gamble). A Wendy's coupon for a free Frosty is a medium of exchange until it expires. After the expiration date, the coupon will only be good for kindling. We can apply this analogy to the cash in your wallet or the money in your checking account. That medium of exchange (the cash) represents potential wealth, but inflation can reduce its value relative to the price of goods. Something similar happened with toxic mortgage-backed securities. Speculators hoped those securities would represent potential wealth, but they lost so much value that it led to the 2008 Great Recession.

A home is (hopefully) a durable good. It provides shelter, security, and a feeling of belonging. However, as the largest share of wealth of most families, it is also a speculative asset. The land on which a home is built provides a means through which households and firms can generate future value. The property could be converted into wealth. If a person buys a home for $200,000 and sells it five years later for $220,000, she could then figure out her gains in wealth after deducting costs for insurance, property tax, and repairs. If she buys a home for $200,000 and sells it five years later for $180,000 then she would be at least 10 percent less wealthy. Regardless of what happens to the monetary value of the house, she would accrue benefits from having shelter for her family, but in financial terms her wealth could grow or shrink simply because of changes in the housing market.

From an economist's point of view, the speculative service of a house is more measurable than any other service it provides. We can forecast the value of a home in a real estate market and even leverage that potential value with a HELOC or another financial scheme. Less measurable to an economist are the unpriced benefits of living in a home: the security of owning a place to live and forming relationships with neighbors; the fun of making home improvements; the ability to grow a garden, brew a home ale, or host barbeques with friends. These are not market transactions, so they have no price. A smart realtor might increase the price to account for some of these services, but such factors are subjective. The price movements observed by economists come primarily from how well the land on which the house was built continued to provide speculative value. The price of a house built in an inner-ring suburb may decline as wealthier families move to a suburb farther out, even if the house itself is in pristine condition and "worth" every penny the initial buyer put into it.

In the past, home values were linked to factors like the supply of available homes, good schools, reliable utilities, or proximity to employment centers. Now investment firms engage in real estate speculation, believing that they can buy a house this year and sell it next year for a profit. That is because demand for homes is *inelastic*, which means that people will always want to buy houses because there are so few viable substitutes. By contrast, demand for potato chips would be *elastic* because the buyer has so many options (e.g., corn chips).

Because demand for houses is inelastic, renting an apartment or buying a condo are often viewed as inferior alternatives. Therefore, large-scale investors assume there will always be demand for houses, and that drives up the price. This mentality partially fueled the rise in home prices between 1997 and 2007. Economist Robert Shiller described what happened in that period as *irrational exuberance* because investors chased increasingly expensive assets and therefore fueled a price boom with their own speculative demand. As prices rise, investors expect that price will continue going up, which leads them to buy more of the asset and sell later. This further increases demand and therefore increases the price. The inflationary cycle might cause a precarious bubble, but in the short term it marginalizes middle- and low-income families from the real estate market. Landowners and landlords need not worry so much about renters' rights, maintenance, or other occupation costs; instead, they can let the house sit empty and assume that they will profit from continued speculation.

How much of the housing market is subject to this irrational exuberance? In 2021, according to the National Association of Realtors, 15 percent of all single-family dwellings purchased in the United States were purchased by institutional investors. In 2022, that number for the state of Texas was 30 percent. Other sunbelt states like Georgia, Arizona, and Oklahoma had similar rates of institutional home buying. According to a US Housing and Urban Development estimate, institutional investors owned about seven hundred thousand single family homes as of August 2022. Spread across a total volume of about 144 million homes, that number seems paltry, but the rate of institutional home buying impacts current trends far more than total volume. According to the Federal Reserve, there were 869,000 actively listed homes in the US in

June 2024. Obviously, institutional investors did not buy all those listings, but we can see how a few thousand purchases can shift the demand curve a great deal. Because housing is an inelastic good, even small increases in home prices can trigger broad and rapid home price inflation. The culprit for this inflation is not renters' or homeowners' Covid relief checks.

Institutional investors have another advantage over average Americans: They have access to the Federal Reserve's banking window. This means they can take out loans from the Fed at a lower interest and then lend that money at a higher rate. Between 2008 and 2015, and between 2020 to 2022, the effective rate at the Fed's banking window was essentially zero. The Fed made this cheap money available on the assumption that banks would lend the money to businesses and other banks who would in turn put that money to productive economic use. But since 2008, many lenders chose to hold that money in reserves, or to seek less risky and less productive investments. Importantly, the people and institutions who borrow from the Fed can do so at a *much lower interest rate cost* than small-scale home buyers, individual households, and small- to mid-size firms. When was the last time you were able to secure a loan with an interest rate of 0.11 percent?[8]

When the Federal Reserve enacts stimulus measures during a recession or economic shock, as it did in 2008 and 2020, banks and institutional investors can access liquidity at lower interest rates while households must purchase homes at a higher retail interest rate. If there is a recession, then it is risky for them to lend to firms because so many are contracting or going bankrupt. Stock markets are just as volatile in recessionary periods. Investing in real estate, therefore, can be a good option—if it is held over a prolonged period. You can see how this economic policy drives inequality in the US; the wealthy institutional actors in the housing market play by rules that do not apply to average Americans.

And that is not all. During the 2007-2008 financial crisis, which originated in the housing sector, the Federal Reserve responded by dumping boatloads of money into banks. This was probably necessary to avoid another Great Depression, but we should remember that these actions benefited the wealthiest Americans far more than middle- and lower-income Americans. Then, during the 2020 Covid-19 pandemic, the Fed initiated another round of monetary stimulus, which mostly went to the banks. The amount? About $2.4 trillion, according to the Federal Reserve's asset balance sheet. That amount was four times the total amount of household income held by the poorest 20 percent of Americans in 2020 ($607 billion), according to the US Census Bureau. It is true that the government sent pandemic relief payments to Americans, but the total amount of that support pales in comparison to the flood of liquidity the Fed pumped into banks and firms. Anyone who says that fiscal stimulus delivered to low-income households was inflationary is not telling the truth. The amount received by that population was almost nothing compared to the government support received by banks and large companies.

As that money from the Fed flowed to banks and large financial firms like Berkshire Hathaway, institutional real estate speculators could use the capital to purchase houses and rent them, knowing that the property value would increase. As a result, companies like Berkshire Hathaway gained price control of the rental market. They now own the land. They can evict people who struggle to pay rent. They can leave homes vacant, decreasing the potential supply of rental housing. To make matters worse, consolidation in the banking and finance sectors (see figure 2-3) means that fewer banks and firms control the real estate market.

Larger firms have a monopolistic advantage. They can make profits at much lower costs than smaller firms. Think about Walmart in the retail sector. This massive company can undercut the price of products by pressuring suppliers to accept lower payments. Because they control freight transportation, they can reduce the cost of moving products. Smaller firms do not have these advantages. Banking and finance operate similarly. It is extremely difficult to open a bank. Banks need accountants, lawyers, experts in regulation, ATMs, and a lot of capital to provide cash or savings for borrowers and depositors. So, it is cheaper for larger banks to do business than smaller banks. As a result, smaller banks are going out of business.

Because real estate has become a financial and *speculative* market instead of a *housing* market, it provides advantages for the big guys. The more property Berkshire and Goldman Sachs buy, the cheaper it is for them to speculate. The smaller real estate firms that are trying to provide housing to individuals and families will find it harder to stay in the market. Will the speculators be the only survivors? That would be a profoundly disturbing result.

. As mentioned above, the Federal Reserve gave banks and financial firms $2.4 trillion dollars. They used this capital, at least in part, to capture real estate markets. This money could have gone to providing liquidity to low- or middle-income households.

Yet another policy design has fueled rampant real estate speculation. Until recently, the Federal Reserve kept lending rates low for over a decade (2009 to 2022). This meant that some people could secure home loans at low interest rates, typically between 3 to

5 percent. However, that had a perverse impact. Lower rates should make housing more affordable for *everyone,* but low rates often apply only to people who have good credit, which often excludes people who are lower on the economic ladder. Credit ratings agencies have been around since at least 1841, but the nationalized credit score we all know and despise today was created by the Fair Isaac Corporation (FICO), a company founded in 1956 that went public in 1987. The rise of national credit ratings agencies, such as Experian, came after decades of consolidation among credit rating agencies, until only the big three remained. A mostly well-intentioned system metastasized into a method by which those with money can exclude those without it from the benefits of the modern economy.

The inequalities built into the credit rating system directly impact the housing sector. Lower rates set by the Fed made land speculation easier for the rich. Institutional buyers usually have access to the Federal Reserve's discount borrowing window, but even if they do not have that access, businesses with good credit can secure cheap loans with which to buy more housing.

These realities present two dangers. First, a flood of speculative money prices people out of a house, which is a basic necessity. That could drive more people closer to destitution, the logical extreme being homelessness. The second danger is a return to barter. When shelter becomes unaffordable for many people, the value of money itself may be called into question. If significant portions of the population cannot maintain the stability of shelter, they might turn to exchanging real goods and services for dwellings. For example, a handyman might agree to work in exchange for rent. This arrangement might work until either the handyman or the property owner decides to change the agreement. If prior trust does not exist, exploitation and/or violence can ensue.

This perfect storm of speculative money and constrained housing supply did not just spin itself into existence. Almost a century of market forces, interacting with and compounded by community forces, put us in the current situation.

Market Forces: Zoning

How did the American real estate landscape become so dominated by single-family housing? We can trace this trend to the city of Euclid, Ohio in early 1922. The citizens of Euclid decided they wanted to pass restrictive laws that specified the kinds of houses and businesses that could and could not be built in their town. This being the 1920s, there was a strong undercurrent of racism and classism behind the decisions, but there were also valid reasons for restrictive zoning. For instance, without laws that restricted noise and air pollution to nonresidential parts of town, businesses could have placed, say, a paper mill next to a previously peaceful family neighborhood. People in the neighborhood would have had no legal recourse. For readers who have not experienced the joys of living near a paper mill, imagine a neighborhood that smells like burnt cabbages. Or imagine that the house next to yours is turned into a laundromat and the operator dumps cleaning chemicals into the alley behind your back door.

Our point is that Euclidean zoning did not always have nefarious or cruel motivations. Restrictive zoning was used to exclude people of color and the poor, but zoning laws were also used to prevent the entry of dangerous or undesirable industries into residential neighborhoods.

Local zoning laws around the nation gradually became more restrictive. In addition to designating residential, commercial, or industrial zones, cities began to "micromanage" who could build what and where. For instance, cities set limits on the number of dwelling units per lot, thereby preventing the construction of a small rental unit next to the main house. Many cities prevented people from building apartments above retail or office spaces, a practice that had been normal in American towns and cities in the nineteenth century. By the 1950s, land owners had to comply with minimum parking requirements for commercial areas, restrictions on house sizes, and expensive fire suppression systems.

These specific requirements often made sense at the micro level, but a century of zoning laws has squeezed the housing market into two physical locations. Although some cities and counties have relaxed zoning laws, Americans usually must choose between a single-family detached home or a large apartment complex. In both cases, their homes could be quite far from their jobs or the places where they enjoy spending free time.

There has been a recent resurgence in the desire to put housing units above commercial space, but these buildings are often subject to commercial building codes that drive up the cost of construction. That forces developers to build large projects that can offer the most return on investment. And *that* typically means luxury housing.

Market Forces: Land As a Speculative Tool

The power of zoning laws to limit residential construction to certain parts of a city restricts the nominal freedom of the housing market to meet demand for new housing. In the luxury apartment example, we see that the provision of housing driven by market forces has produced a situation in which demand rises even as zoning laws constrain supply. Instead of meeting the demand for affordable housing by increasing supply, real estate developers now use land as a speculative tool. To make a profit, they team up with investment banks and venture capital speculators who skim their fees off the top and then sell the new building. After the developers take their cut, the banks own an asset that will, they assume, only appreciate. If it does not, they can write off the depreciation as a loss for tax purposes and sell the lot again. They hope. This demonstrates one of the problems with speculation: For every winner there is at least one loser.

There is a role for speculation. Any investment, including saving for retirement, involves some degree of speculation. Some types are safer than others. A safer form of speculation would, at least for now, be the purchase of US Treasury bonds. We expect the US government to exist and pay what it owes; but even that involves speculation. At the time this book is going to press, President Trump's imposition of tariffs and the possible expansion of the US deficit caused by proposed tax cuts is making Treasury bonds seem less safe. So, even a speculation that seems safe is not always safe in hindsight. Someone who purchased mortgage-backed securities in 2006 was told by credible rating agencies (raise a glass to Moody's) that these investments were safe. People who deposited more than the FDIC $250,000 insurance limit in Silicon Valley Bank in 2023 lost what they believed was a safe bet. An example of an extremely risky form of speculation would be to put money into a "meme coin" or a slot machine.

Massive real estate speculation occurred during the early- to mid-2000s. Investors found that if you slice and dice thousands of mortgages and then repackage them into one asset (a bit like making sausage), one can generate a larger store of value while simultaneously speculating in the broader US monetary system. Because most mortgage borrowers pay off their debt, an asset made of ten thousand mortgages will still return a substantial revenue even if 1 percent of those mortgages end up in default. But that bet assumed that a large number of borrowers would not default on their house loans. That assumption proved false starting in late 2007 and early 2008, at which point about 5 percent of housing assets became distressed. A major financial crisis promptly followed because investment banks were not able to maintain healthy balance sheets.

The root problem of real estate speculation is that it is easier for financial institutions to buy land than to make good investments in businesses or ventures. This does not mean that the people who run financial institutions lack intelligence; rather, it means that real estate is a surer and simpler bet compared to trying to choose an investment in, for example, a tech startup without adequate information. For example, banks typically buy up large plots of land on the edges of cities and then plop a gas station on the corner. The gas station, even if it does not turn a profit, satisfies the owner's legal requirement to improve the property, which changes the zoning classification. In a few years, when the growth of the city reaches the rural gas station, the investors knock down the gas station and then build a housing subdivision or a strip mall or some combination of the two. The investor's land finally yields a profit.

The example described above demonstrates how institutional investors can profit from speculation rather than from investing. What is the difference? The primary distinction is that, in the case of speculation, the investors' objective is to maximize profit by holding land rather than utilizing it to serve the needs of the broader population. The outcome of this type of speculation is the artificial constriction of housing supply, which drives up prices for average people.

Or consider the example of Airbnb. What was supposed to be a way to rent out an extra property when the owners were not using it morphed into a global operation in which more single-family homes are bought solely for the purpose of short-term rentals. This practice removes single-family residences from the housing market, which drives up the prices of the remaining homes. That can have negative effects on the community. Short-term rental agreements mean that permanent residents are unable to know their neighbors. Usually, the property owner has no incentive to spend money on anything beyond minimal upkeep. The owner also has no real investment in the social capital of the neighborhood.

These factors, which are designed to benefit institutional investors, increase the inequality gap in the housing market and across all of society. The largest profits from real estate speculation come from the luxury and higher-end housing sectors, so speculators tend to hold on to land for those types of homes, which is what developers want to build. Meanwhile, starter homes and lower-end projects languish or get bought by rent-seekers who want to list properties on Airbnb. These practices force many lower-income prospective homebuyers into mobile homes. Over the last ten years, the average price of a single-width mobile home nearly doubled.[9]

These price increases occurred simultaneously with a rising supply of mobile homes, as measured by total units shipped nationwide. In 2020, approximately 90,000 mobile homes were shipped in the US. That number increased to about 100,000 in 2021 and up again to 110,000 in 2022. Nevertheless, the prices increased during those years. One would expect that a supply increase would drive down prices or at least slow the rise in prices. That has not been observed across the country. What we see is a spillover effect; people who cannot afford a single-family home but do not want to rent might be inclined to buy a mobile home.

In a monetary sense, mobile homes have two big drawbacks. The house itself, due to its lower quality, does not store value the way regular houses do. Second, when they are placed in mobile home parks, as is usually the case, the house sits on land owned by another person or company, which further reduces the home's store of value. This is not to say no one should buy or live in a mobile home. Our point is that increasing numbers of average Americans find themselves in a hostile housing market, which pushes them to choose between a financially poor substitute for a fixed-foundation house. Many need to buy mobile homes, which for the reasons described above, further increases inequality. The other option is to rent. Speaking of rent . . .

Market Forces: The Rent Is Too Damn High

Over the last decade, as stated earlier, the Federal Reserve offered loans at rock bottom rates to investment firms. These firms used a lot of the money to speculate in real estate markets across America, buying cheap land on the periphery, or buying post-industrial properties in city centers. Real estate developers made decisions whether to build or not based on how they could make the most money, regardless of the demand for affordable dwellings. In addition, zoning laws in most municipalities forced builders to construct new housing in sprawling subdivisions or build single-use apartment buildings. This led to the rise of luxury apartment buildings in downtowns across America over the last decade.

Two predictable problems emerged. First, luxury apartments do not increase the supply of affordable housing, so the demand for housing among average citizens has remained unchanged. Some local governments require that a certain percentage of units be marketed to low-income tenants, but this number is not enough to have a significant influence on lowering rents for less-wealthy renters, and the discount afforded to the low-income renters is often passed on to those paying "fair market" rates. This prices out some people in the middle who may have been able to afford rent if the landlords did not pass the cost of government support for low-income renters onto their shoulders. Many people still find themselves paying higher rent than they should be.

Second, luxury housing drives up costs for everyone else. Fewer people can afford to rent a luxury apartment, which increases the number of vacant units. In response, management companies typically raise rents rather than lower them. For an apartment owner, the profit margin for *rented* apartments could be quite high, but the owner of the building could suffer losses depending on how many vacant units there are. This situation is eerily like what is happening with the vast numbers of unoccupied commercial office spaces in the US, a situation caused by the post-pandemic work-from-home revolution. We could see bad loans and crashing investment returns in the commercial real estate sector. All this is undermining the financial sector and discouraging developers from building affordable apartments. People who make less than six figures will struggle to find a place to live.

There is more. The lack of regulation has allowed property owners to coordinate rent prices on a regional basis, thus eliminating the competition that helps to reduce rent prices. Some companies have billed their software programs as a way for property owners to index their rents to regional trends.[10] These programs provide property owners and managers with two advantages. First, the companies use data that is not available to renters; only property owners have access to that information. This access to what economists call "perfect information" gives the property owners a major advantage over renters. The property managers know which units are available at any given time and the proposed rate. Thus, they can set their rental rates at the most profitable levels for themselves. Meanwhile, the renters must guess where to find the best rental price.

Moreover, these programs provide property owners with algorithms to set rents as high as statistically possible, often on a unit-by-unit basis. For example, rather than advertise a set rate of $800 per month for similar apartments in each complex, the leasing office can take the income data of prospective renters, run it through the algorithm, and then quote the renter the most expensive rate he or she can pay.

If you think this sounds like an exploitative business practice, you are not alone. In August 2024, the US Justice Department sued a company operating in numerous states for implementing a "pricing scheme that harms millions of American renters."[11] In short, landlords uploaded privately disclosed financial data from renters, sharing it with other landlords. The program's algorithm determined the maximum rent the landlord could charge. The algorithm took into account that some renters would not be able to pay the higher amount and provided the landlord with an "appropriate" vacancy rate at which the landlord could still maximize profits. The program did not consider the process of pushing some tenants into homelessness. That is just the cost of doing business.

This sort of exploitation comes with a high-tech veneer, but in other cases the exploitation of renters happens with the old-fashioned grime of burst water pipes and missing sheetrock. In Tulsa, Oklahoma, an out-of-state management company purchased a 160-unit apartment complex sometime in the 2010s. The property manager, despite charging above-market rates, refused to make repairs. Many units lacked proper sheetrock and insulation, increasing fire risk. When a polar vortex brought subzero temperatures to Tulsa in early 2021, the units proved to be unsafe for human habitation. Water pipes burst in uninsulated units, further damaging the structure of the buildings. Rather than repair the damage, or even manage the problem, the company simply ran up a $100,000 water bill with the city, which they never paid. Eventually, the city declared all six hundred units to be uninhabitable. The tenants were forced to move out.[12]

These anecdotes do not necessarily represent statistical averages; however, in the current rental environment, with home prices sky-high and affordable rent alternatives sorely lacking, real estate management companies have no incentive to lower rent prices or provide adequate services to renters. Every year, Americans are forced to rent at higher rates in exchange for lower quality housing. We should not be surprised if Americans feel like they are prey for rent-seeking predators. We should not be surprised if they feel frustration toward those in charge, leaders who do not care about their plight and instead actively collude with the property owners and institutional speculators who promulgate the average person's misery.

Community Forces: Elite Capture of Local Government

Real estate developers often create the false impression that they are interested in helping communities when they present projects to land covenants and homeowners' associations. This makes sense because developers want to make sure that the zoning codes and municipal enforcement are friendly to them. They also have every incentive to invest in politicians. They have the cash to pump up the campaign of someone who wishes to perpetuate a system that benefits developers.

The influence of wealthy developers on local politicians also reflects the outsize influence of wealthy people and corporations at the state and national levels. Research published by Princeton

University showed that policy is shaped by those with money and influence. "When Americans with different income levels differ in their policy preferences, actual policy outcomes strongly reflect the preferences of the most affluent but bear virtually no relationship to the preferences of poor or middle income Americans," wrote Martin Gilens, the study's author. "This vast discrepancy in government responsiveness to citizens with different incomes stands in stark contrast to the ideal of political equality that Americans hold dear."[13]

At local and state levels, the "elite capture" of governments has shaped housing and development policies. The policies lead to urban planning that envisions expensive, sprawling models of development. As the American model of city planning moved away from mixed-use buildings, it forced a mostly binary choice on buyers: either a single-family detached home or an apartment. This model made home builders and developers fantastic amounts of money. Those same groups then had the funds and time to go into local politics, or to lobby the politicians, thus ensuring their model of urban development would continue uninterrupted.

As these neoliberal urban development models spread across the US (since the 1950s and 1960s), they eroded social cohesion. The decline of community life in America has many causes, but one is the suburbanization of America. In a 2020 article in *The Atlantic*, David Brooks states this point eloquently.

> Over the past two generations, the physical space separating nuclear families has widened. Before, sisters-in-law shouted greetings across the street at each other from their porches. Kids would dash from home to home and eat out of whoever's fridge was closest by. But lawns have grown more expansive and porch life has declined,

creating a buffer of space that separates the house and family from anyone else. . . . Married people are less likely to visit parents and siblings, and less inclined to help them do chores or offer emotional support. A code of family self-sufficiency prevails: Mom, Dad, and the kids are on their own, with a barrier around their island home.[14]

As this post-World War II model unfolded, people who could afford it searched for some way to replace a lost sense of community. And in their confusion, they created cities within cities. They are called homeowners' associations.

Community Forces: The HOA Is Not Your Friend

Homeowners' associations are not *inherently* evil, especially when they involve condominiums or townhouses. When people share walls and roofs and utilities, a third-party legal structure is a *necessary* evil. HOAs are helpful for managing physical structures. The problem, however, is that these legal entities have become tools of control and commodification. The HOA began as a form of managing collective maintenance, but they have become institutions for social control.

A homeowners' association is a legal mechanism that allows a group of people to pool resources and money to maintain shared physical property. As with corporations, HOAs were intended to be legal vehicles for performing a specific and real-world function. Over the years, they have become mechanisms for controlling the physical spaces of a neighborhood, even in neighborhoods where every building is a single-family detached house. HOAs do not represent a niche market. About 30 percent of Americans live in a community with some kind of association, typically an HOA.[15] This results in enforced conformity labeled as a "community." In this way, real estate speculation has financed the commodification of wrong values on every living space in America.

What is the price of being a member of a community? According to national data, the average cost is $170 per month, if one lives under the authority of an HOA. That number varies wildly depending on the location. Some low-cost areas report monthly fees as low as $50 per month, while others go as high as $1000 per month. The market has attempted to price these services into homeowners' associations. Families pay fees to a group that ensures lawns are mowed, trees are trimmed, and the general look and feel of the neighborhood is up to code. HOAs create a microgovernment within a city government to make and enforce policies. The fees can be steep, so homeowners must believe that their contributions will produce a financial return, or at least prevent a loss. That is the price of looking out for your elderly neighbor or having a neighborhood full of kids with whom your children can play.

HOAs may also provide another service that real estate speculation also provides: pricing out the "undesirables." HOAs can place a financial barrier around higher income neighbors because lower income families may not have the money to meet stringent requirements. HOAs can also harass problem neighbors who commit minor violations, driving them out. Instead of respecting a family's choice of how to landscape their home, for example, the HOA might impose a rigid set of legal requirements enforced by the loudest and most noxious members of a community. The result, which is a commodification of relationships, creates a "vacuum of neighborly values" that destabilizes authentic neighborhood relationships.

Insidiously, the influence of an HOA fuels housing speculation. The point of the HOA is not just to enforce norms and exclude undesirables; it is also designed to ensure that house prices keep rising. As average home prices increase in a region, property taxes increase. Public schools in the US are usually funded by property taxes. In many school districts, about 95 percent of each homeowner's property tax goes to the local school system. In areas with high house prices, schools receive more money. Because families want their kids to go to well-funded schools, they try to live in districts with expensive housing, which increases demand for homes in those districts and further increases the value of the houses. This means that wealthier families with more expensive homes get better schools, which drives up the value of their homes. The poor families end up with lower quality education *and* declining property values. This is yet another example of how policy designs, even at the local level, can perpetuate or worsen inequality.

Pathways to a Better Economy

Policies that create housing inequality, and therefore overall inequality, were intentionally designed. That means they can be *redesigned.* Inequality is not a fate.

There are two pathways forward. One empowers individuals, associations, and communities to tackle systemic economic inequality. These are *grassroots groups,* a term we will use a lot in this book. The other pathway encourages policymakers to design laws and regulations that are fair for average Americans. When we use the term *policymakers,* we do not refer only to elected officials. Our definition of a policymaker includes those who serve as executives in nonprofits or in the private sector. A policymaker can influence the formation of public policy. These two avenues—grassroots groups and policymakers—are not mutually exclusive. We hope that people in both categories will work together to reduce inequality.

Paths for People

Local government could be the best place for grassroots groups to make a difference. City council members do not represent many people, but these elected officials are often more accessible to local citizens than, for example, a state or federal official. So, a grassroots group of homebuyers and renters, if they work together, can have a strong influence on a city council member or county commissioner. Here are a few possibilities.

First, grassroots groups can request local politicians to relax or remove restrictive zoning codes. As mentioned earlier, zoning codes mostly serve to make property more expensive rather than keeping undesirable businesses out of neighborhoods. Grassroots groups can respect the need to keep heavy industries, for example, out of residential areas; but they can also push local elected officials to remove or adjust setback requirements and single-family zoning requirements. Doing so would quickly allow for a large amount of new home construction. An increased supply of housing should lower prices for average income earners.

Second, grassroots groups can pressure local elected officials to pass city codes that explicitly forbid the establishment of homeowners' associations or land ownership covenants, which drive up housing prices. Exceptions can be made for dwellings that share walls or roofs (e.g., condominiums and townhomes).

Third, grassroots groups should push local officials to change city zoning codes and commercial building codes in ways that would allow businesses to convert parking lots into housing units. People often underestimate how much of a city's area is occupied by large and often empty parking lots.

Fourth, grassroots groups can persuade city officials to require all new residential lots to be subdivided. This would force developers to design smaller, more affordable residential lots, thereby incentivizing builders to build more houses. This is not an overly complicated request. Some local real estate developers who want to sell more houses might support it. A real-world example of this plan is in Smyrna, Delaware. In 2004, a real estate developer purchased 115 acres, with plans to put in a traditional single-family subdivision with 430 homes. The plans got shelved in 2008 and the land remained vacant for seventeen years. In 2021, a new developer restarted the project. This time, the town council wanted to see more units, to help with housing affordability, so they used the planned village community model. As a result, they nearly doubled the number of units to 709. The units included a mix of detached houses and townhomes. This small win did not completely solve Delaware's housing affordability crunch, but it represents what can be done at the local level to address macro issues that seem overwhelming.[16]

Fifth, we encourage citizens to think about forming a homebuyers' union. This is exactly what it sounds like: A collection of individuals within a geographic area agrees to only buy houses that are priced within a specific range. We recognize that this idea is a tall order to implement. It would require all prospective homebuyers *to find each other* and then agree to only buy houses within a specific price range. We also know that any type of formal union membership, including in workplaces, requires the complete commitment of an entire group of people. Nevertheless, the idea is valid. A homebuyers' union would move buying power away from sellers and back to a middle point between sellers and buyers.

We do not want to create an impression that such efforts would be easy. The current system of land speculation and elite capture limits the options for grassroots groups. But with patience, commitment, and leadership, grassroots groups can leverage economically sound solutions to shift supply and demand curves in ways that benefit average Americans.

Pathways for Policymakers

Our proposal for policymakers, at least those who care about the citizens they serve, is this: require residential properties to be owned by human beings and not legal entities. This would prevent institutional real estate speculation. This recommendation could be implemented at the local, state, or national level. It would not require an extensive government program, and it would not be expensive to implement.

The immediate effect of this proposal would potentially free up an estimated forty-four million housing units, including single-family homes and apartments, that are owned by institutional speculators of some type.[17] In addition to those forty-four million residences, there are about six million residential properties listed as short-term rentals on websites like Airbnb and Vrbo. That means that about fifty million housing units in the US are tied up as rentals, a remarkable number. With that type of control on housing supply, rental costs and home prices increase, thus increasing the difficulty of low- and middle-income citizens who need affordable housing.

The remedy for the inefficiency of a monopolist economy is price controls. Economists decry the use of price controls in every ECON 101 textbook, *except* in the case of a monopolistic market. In those cases, price regulations can restore some amount of efficiency and surplus back to the consumer, while still providing a sufficient market supply. A targeted quota would not disrupt "the efficient market" because the real estate market is not perfectly competitive, as we have shown. Economists commonly agree that it is beneficial to regulate monopolies in utility and communications markets (e.g., cable). So, policymakers only need to recognize that land and housing sectors also need price controls. This can be done without hurting honest investors (as opposed to institutional speculators).

By requiring residential housing to be owned by human beings rather than institutional speculators, policymakers would significantly reduce artificially driven price increases in the real estate market. *Individuals* still might "flip houses," but not on the scale that billion dollar corporations would. In simple economic terms, this solution would increase the supply of houses and therefore decrease prices. Policymakers could effectively remove the gamblers from the pee-wee football game.

We recognize that this plan would hurt those who already own property, because they might see a decline in the value of their houses, but do we really want a housing market that is driven by speculation? Would it not be better for property owners to live in a comfortable and secure location, a true community? A targeted quota would restore the housing market to the provision of family homes and away from the services of speculation.

We also recognize that this policy would need to be adopted on a national level. As stated earlier, housing tends to be an inelastic good, so even a marginal price change, up or down, tends to have strong effects on prices outside a local market. Therefore, even if new policies pushed only half the forty-four million institutionally owned rental units into the open market, average national prices could fall considerably. The coordination of a national policy would be challenging because states have legal authority to control commerce within their borders. Nevertheless, we believe that policymakers should be there to help the people who elected them; thus, they should search for ways to overcome these obstacles.

Another ambitious option for policymakers would be to replicate a public housing effort that was implemented by the government of Vienna, Austria between the World Wars. Starting in the early 1920s, the city government recognized the serious housing shortfall in the city. They cared enough about the citizens to develop and implement a plan. The city built publicly owned apartment buildings that offered rents at set prices. Instead of taking the route pursued in the United States, Vienna's government did not place an income cap on those who wanted to live in these apartment buildings. When designing the buildings, the city elevated the importance of aesthetics. They included amenities that would attract a mix of income levels. World War II imposed a pause on construction, but when the war ended in 1945, the city government doubled down on the interwar project. Today, the City of Vienna owns about 25 percent of the housing units, making it one of the most affordable cities in Europe.

Any town or city in America could implement such a program. The home construction efforts would not need to be especially big to have a significant effect on the local housing market. If the city government could act as a counterweight to the pricing power currently held by institutional speculators, local housing markets would move toward a competitive equilibrium, bringing down both rents and home prices.

Doing nothing to lower housing costs is a horrible option. In 1871, the cost of rent in Paris played a role in sparking a revolutionary moment. France was in the process of losing the Franco-Prussian War and establishing the Second Republic. The new government passed a law requiring Parisians to pay missed rents from when the Prussians had the city under siege. This, understandably, made a lot of Parisians mad. The people of Paris drove out government forces and set up the Paris Commune.

Housing alone will not push the United States into a revolution or cause political violence. However, overpriced housing is one factor that intensifies the accurate perception that insular elites conspire with political leaders to unfairly set prices. The benefits of this system are not diffuse; rather, they are funneled to the top of the wealth pyramid and therefore enjoyed by few.

When a system of political economy loses the confidence of the people who must carry on with their lives within a set of increasingly rigged rules, the frustration of those people will reach a boiling point. They will either express this frustration at the ballot box or through other means.

CHAPTER 4

Birth, Death, and Taxes

How can we discuss inequality without discussing three topics that we all inevitably deal with? It is time to wade into the turbulent waters of children, dying, and taxation.

Objections to taxation are quite common. Some are reasonable: "I'm over-taxed." Some are tenuous: "I'm double taxed." Some are outright ridiculous: "Taxation is theft." In all these statements, we can see two common but false assumptions: paying taxes does not produce anything of value and citizens never get anything in return.

There are anecdotal examples of wasteful taxation. One is the F-35 Joint Strike Fighter boondoggle. The US Government Accounting Office (GAO), in 2023, estimated "it will cost nearly $1.7 trillion to buy, operate, and sustain the aircraft and systems over its lifetime." However, "the F-35 program continues to experience schedule delays, cost growth, and late deliveries." The GAO added that "the F-35 program's total procurement costs have increased by $13.4 billion since the last cost estimate in 2019."[18]

It is also fair to argue that many taxpayers do not directly benefit from school systems or fire departments. Teachers and firefighters do a brilliant job, often for low pay, but many people complain that they must pay taxes for these services even if they do not have kids in school and even if their houses never catch fire. In what ways do taxpayers without kids benefit from educating the next generation of citizens? Should all taxpayers be required to pay for fire stations full of trained professionals who drive shiny red trucks to places where combustion is out of control?

Many people might object to our arguments in this chapter, assuming that we are "pro-taxation." That is not our point. We are saying that paying taxes, even when some individuals do not receive direct benefits, is important for overall social well-being. In many cases, this means that our neighbors with kids will benefit from public schools, that a neighbor with a house on fire will benefit from a prompt response by the fire department, or that a neighbor who drives a semi-truck for a living will benefit from a publicly funded highway system. Where would Amazon be without publicly funded roads? Paying taxes is, in principle, a way for citizens and businesses to bond together to provide funding for projects and services that are important for everyone—for the society in which we live.

Most people agree with these simple principles. The hard part is deciding which public projects to fund and who should pay higher or lower tax rates. Tax rates were not built into the laws of nature, so those questions require the hard work of legislation, or what the Founders called "taxation *with* representation." Unfortunately, lawmakers often design taxation in ways that benefit the wealthiest sectors of society to the detriment of middle and lower classes. In this chapter we report on some often overlooked ways that the fabulously rich use the US tax code to entrench their position of economic primacy.

Generational Economic Mobility

We, the authors, do not accept a deterministic argument that people end up good, bad, or otherwise solely as a product of birth and environment. Individual choices matter, especially as each person reaches an age of maturity. That said, we do believe that three factors—biological (nature), parenting (nurture), and economic—*influence* who each person becomes, for good or ill.

Biology profoundly impacts how a person experiences life. The normal length of a pregnancy is forty weeks. This initial phase of life impacts the growth and development of a person until death. During pregnancy, the mother could suffer the negative impacts of air and water pollution, or she could make poor personal choices like drug use, or she could lack access to proper prenatal care. Genetic factors can play a significant role in the biological formation of growth of a person. But biology is not the focus of this book.

Second, parenting styles certainly make a difference in a person's growth and development. Parenting (the nurture factor) might involve dietary habits, religious upbringing, and educational choices. But parenting is also not the focus of this book, so we will move on to the economic factors that affect the well-being of each generation.

The outcome of a person's life is strongly influenced by the economic conditions into which he or she is born. In the United States today, parental income has a near-deterministic impact on the economic future of a child. Reliable studies indicate that a child's ZIP code influences future lifetime earnings more than any other factor.

Before you throw this book across the room because you know someone who grew up poor and ended up rich, please remember that socioeconomic research deals with averages and the statistical significance of broad, community-level data. Exceptions to every rule exist. Some people break out of poverty traps and some kids born to well-off families can end up penniless. These anomalous cases are notable because they are *exceptions*. However, the statistics are valid. An American child will usually end up making roughly the same income as his or her parents. Exhaustive research of US tax data has found conclusively that children born in the 1980s who were in the poorest quintiles usually remained as poor as their parents when they became adults. Likewise, kids born to the richest 20 percent of Americans rarely fell below their parents' levels of wealth.[19]

This is a hard reality to face, but the statistics debunk false claims that poverty is always the result of moral failure—bad decisions. There are anecdotal examples of people making bad decisions, but the evidence does not support that overall narrative. If a child grows up in a poor family, it does not mean that the parents somehow failed. The underlying problem, as demonstrated by research, is the degree to which parental income has become the primary determining factor for the economic well-being of younger generations in America. Many parents long to see their kids move up the economic ladder, but the economic traps in which they live prevent them providing opportunities to help their children. And remember that *all* economic classes are becoming poorer in real terms. We are seeing a widespread generational decline.

How Are You Going to Pay for Your Kid?

It is no secret that raising kids is expensive. Even if you rely on a midwife to avoid the high cost of a hospital birth, the little ones will cost a lot of money to feed, clothe, shelter, and educate. According to the USDA, a two-parent family making between $60,000 and $107,000 per year spends about $13,000 a year to care for one child. Poorer families spend less because they do not have the resources. Wealthier families spend more on their children than those with average incomes.

However, lower-income families spend a higher *percentage* of their income on raising kids than wealthy parents. Poor families therefore face a "double bind." To care for their children, they need to cut spending on household items *and* they have less income to invest in their own human capital (e.g., education, job training, etc.). Parents who would like to attend community college in hopes of landing a better-paid job usually cannot afford that dream because of child-care costs. Without financial margin, low-income parents often cannot take advantage of opportunities for economic advancement. This perpetuates long-term economic inequality. Families can become locked in an economic class for generations.

Earlier we discussed the gap between personal income and per-worker GDP. We showed that, since the early 1980s, incomes have declined even as the overall economy grew. About $50 trillion of wealth flowed to the upper economic sectors of society from the lower and middle class sectors. With that situation in mind, we can look at the impact this gap has on *households*. According to the Census Bureau, the average household in the United States comprises 2.6 people. If we look at GDP-per-worker and engaged spending measures, we might reasonably assume that two people in the household are legally able to work. Those two workers would need to earn enough to spend $170,000 in 2024 to participate in the "average spending" levels of the US economy.

The US Census data for 2023 shows a median household income of $80,610. That covers only 48 percent of GDP-per-worker that same year. In other words, the median income of a middle quintile household covers less than half the spending necessary to engage in US economic activity on a per-worker basis. Notice that the gap between household income and per-capita GDP becomes a gaping chasm when compared to wealthier sectors. US Census data reports for 2023 show that the household income at the ninetieth percentile is $316,000, which is well above the level necessary for average engaged spending. This GDP-to-income gap helps to explain the widespread sentiment that everything feels more expensive. This situation is the result of a multi-decade trend of wealthier households getting richer and spending more while the middle class and lower income groups experience the pain of stagnating or declining incomes. Overall economic health numbers like GDP have decoupled from Americans' real income.

The decline of real wages makes it tough to afford children. According to Gallup's annual survey, 64 percent of Americans with children report that they do not want more children because they do not have enough money. Another 12 percent say that economic hardship or the lack of jobs prevents them from having more children. The same survey shows that Americans believe the ideal number of children is 2.7 children.[20] Nevertheless, the birthrate has declined by 11 percent between 1990 and 2024 (according to the

Centers for Disease Control and Prevention). In other words, many families want to have more children, but they cannot afford to do so. Economic inequality is one factor that drives down the size of American's families.

Most parents say they would sacrifice anything for their kids. That is good, because any society where parents cannot or will not sacrifice for their kids will not remain a "society" for long. But if having more kids becomes economically untenable, people will decide to have fewer children. At the macro level, this puts developed economies like the US in a bind. As nations around the world moved from agrarian to industrial systems, the birth rates in those countries plummeted. In 2024, the total fertility rate (TFR) in every industrial country was lower than 2.1 kids per woman, which is considered the minimum to maintain a stable population. At the macroeconomic level, we see that economic inequality is driving people in the industrial world toward extinction.

This trend has happened in part because there is easy access to birth control and family planning. Curiously, as shown in US Census data, poorer communities tend to have slightly higher TFRs than wealthier communities. One reason might be that poorer people lack access to birth control and sexual health education. But there could be a darker reason: Poorer communities have higher rates of infant and child mortality; therefore, some poor families may choose to have more children because they want to increase their chances of seeing at least one or two kids survive to adulthood. Many poor individuals have more children, not because they are cynically pursuing higher welfare benefits, but because they believe (with reason) that at least one child will die an early, tragic death.

I (Ben) can attest to the truth of this assumption. Working

among impoverished communities as an EMT, I often directly witnessed the cheapness of life in places where violence and poor health were shockingly common. Hardly anyone made it to age sixty without a chronic health condition of some kind, and these conditions were often fatal due to a lack of health care. Our emergency ambulances and local emergency rooms served as health clinics for the dispossessed because those people could rarely find standard care elsewhere. I lost count of the number of young men and women whose lives were devastated by street violence or legal and illegal drug use.

The mental health toll of poverty is immense. Poor and marginalized children will grow up with a mentality that life is cheap, and that the wider world is out to get them. They are not entirely wrong. Unfortunately, the economy in which we have raised two-and-a-half generations of Americans communicates that human life is cheap. In that context, the ever-increasing ranks of marginalized people will become more susceptible to radicalization.

Older generations complain that younger generations have been raised the wrong way. These arguments are mostly unconvincing. Kids make mistakes while growing up, and those mistakes often reflect as much on the parents as on the youth. That said, the damage that economic inequality brings to children and young adults, as the research shows, is far more insidious than parenting styles or other cultural factors (e.g., social media). When the broader political economy operates so blatantly in favor of a tiny, dominant class, and when we treat all others as disposable, we should not be surprised by the radicalization of today's politics. Should we really find it all that shocking that so many choose to vote for any bull who promises to wreck the china shop?

Until Death Do You Part (With Inequality)?

Despite claims by longevity experts, health nuts, and technophiles, the pale rider will come for all of us someday. However, the true sorrow that comes from death is not experienced by the dead, but by those left behind.

Recall Marty's family, mourning the loss of a loving father and husband. We blamed this hypothetical death on the pandemic, but other economic factors played a major role. Marty's job came with a health savings account instead of health insurance. His work schedule took from him the time needed to control his diabetes through diet and exercise. Marty did not die at work, but his death left his family with exorbitant bills and a loss of his much needed income, time, and support. Marty's life was worth just as much as his old schoolmate Chad's, but the inequality that plagued Marty all his life followed him to his grave.

We can compare the financial payouts that might have occurred if Chad, Marty, and Jenny had all died a wrongful death, a death caused by crime or negligence. What if our golden boy, Chad, died July 4, 2020 at age fifty-eight, about fifteen years before he planned to retire? Suppose Chad made $280,000 per year at the time of his death. We can also assume that Chad would have received a few raises (3 to 4 percent each) and end-of-year bonuses—if he had not died. In this scenario, economists would calculate the raises and bonuses, forecast the risk of disease or permanent injury that might have kept him from working, and find a lump sum payout to compensate his family for those lost fifteen years of paychecks. The courts, with the help of economists, can help to make Chad's beneficiaries continue living as they had before. The courts and economists might conclude that Chad's death should be valued at $3 million to $4 million.

What about Marty? Right off the bat we see that Marty is "worth less" in death than Chad. His income while he was alive took several hits: the failed small business in the late 1990s, the bankruptcy of the store he managed in the 2000s, and the need to work as a burger joint manager in his late forties. If we assume that Marty was white, and if we use the standard economic criteria that we used in Chad's case, the court system probably would award Marty's family with about $1.1 million. If Marty were a person of color, his lifetime expected earnings would have been lower; therefore, the courts would have awarded about $985,000 to his family.

Finally, there is sweet Jenny. Suppose she also died during the summer of 2020 while living in a multi-generational home with her daughter and granddaughter. Due to her history of low-paying jobs, and due to the loss of jobs during the pandemic, Jenny's lifetime expected earnings would have been dismal. The courts probably would have awarded her daughter and granddaughter $500,000, a paltry amount that includes the household work Jenny did to take care of her family.

We should stress that courts presiding over this kind of compensation for deaths do not make arbitrary decisions about who is more "valuable" than others. These decisions are based on how the overall US economy values the economic activity of certain groups categorized by sex, ethnicity, and class. Courts consider institutional data about how the actual economy operates, which in turn reflects the broader consensus about whose work and lives are most or least valuable in the US political economy. The courts find that highly educated people tend to live longer and gain higher incomes. These factors drive up the "value" of survivors' losses when someone dies. In wrongful death cases, judges consider levels of education as a factor, which means that poorer people are usually "worth less" at death. Minorities, even controlling for economic class and education, tend to live shorter lives and have lower incomes. As a result, judges base their evaluations on systemic inequalities. The data reflects yet another aspect of our rigged system.

It does not need to be this way. Economists have access to a large body of research that could correct the biases (gender wage gap, race wage gap, education wage gap) in the evaluation process; however, the courts ignore the academic research. Even if judges, lawyers, and economists were the most charitable people alive, the system would skew their decisions in ways that reinforce inequality.

Taxing the Poor to Feed the Rich

We have talked about birth and death, so now it is time to talk about taxes. We all pay them: income taxes, sales taxes, property taxes. We pay them on dividends, on retirement income, and on capital gains. If we have an estate worth more than $13.6 million, our survivors will pay taxes on that too. Paying tax is unavoidable, now more than ever. Information technology provides accurate ways to track every penny. That is great for data collection and for analyzing broad trends in the nation's money flow, so people who wish to avoid taxation must be creative.

Any society that wants to operate a modern economy must

collect taxes to pay for the structures and systems that uphold it. Roads must be built and maintained. Electrical, sewer, and clean water systems must be expanded and repaired. The US relies on taxes to pay hundreds of thousands of police officers and thousands of court employees and judges. We need tax revenue to pay teachers who ensure the country has an educated workforce, and we need a tax base that is sufficient to invest in advanced research and development.

But who pays taxes, at what rates, and when? The US has answered those questions in ways that primarily benefit the wealthy and therefore increase inequality. Tax policies profoundly impact the incomes of everyone, and they shape the ability of each economic class to influence political governance. At the federal level, these policies were written by men and women who came from the monied classes to benefit those same classes.

Capital Gains: When Your Money Makes Money

When we think of the term *income,* we usually imagine going to work and bringing home a paycheck. We also recognize that income can come from business profit. In addition, the government defines a third primary income stream as "capital gains." A person who makes money from the sale of an asset or investment receives capital gains income. The person is not taxed on the money invested; she is only taxed on the profit (gains) from the investment.

The US government, at the time of this writing, only taxes capital gains above a certain amount. For example, if you spent fifty dollars on a rare collectible that you found at a thrift store and then sold it for $100, you would have gained fifty dollars on a capital investment of fifty dollars. If you earn less than $47,000 as a single taxpayer or $94,000 for a couple filing jointly, the fifty bucks in profit would not be subject to capital gains taxation. If you made more than those amounts, you would *technically* be liable to pay a 15 percent tax on the profit, or about $7.50. Single people who make more than $518,000 and married people who file jointly and have a total income of more than $583,000 would pay a 20 percent capital gains tax.

Similarly, if a person makes an investment and takes a loss, then that capital loss can be written off for tax purposes, offsetting any gains earned from other investments that made money. There is also a distinction between short- and long-term capital gains. Overall, the tax system is set up to favor capital investment. That sounds positive, at least on paper. We want investors to take risks and to make new economic investments. However, many investors make money from high-frequency stock trading, which does not build factories, open new businesses, or create jobs. So, why should profits from capital investments be taxed at a lower rate than income earned through hard work?

Here we run into a semantic issue. In economics jargon, a tax policy is *progressive* if the amount paid gets progressively larger as the amount of capital gains goes up. By contrast, and confusingly for public debate, a tax policy is *regressive* when the amount paid eats up a higher share (or percentage) of the payer's investment gains than a wealthier person. A middle-class couple earning $100,000 per year might fall into the 25 percent tax bracket (for income earned by work), but a wealthy investor might make $5 million on an investment and pay at most 20 percent on the capital gains. The middle-class couple would pay fewer dollars, but they would pay *a higher share* of their hard-earned income on taxes than the wealthy investor. The tax burden is heavier for the working couple than for the wealthy investor.

So how does this system of selective taxation drive inequality? It serves to ensure that the rich pay a much lower effective tax rate (as a percentage of income) than everyone else. Most people in the top 1 percent pay effective rates of around 15 percent (or less) in federal income taxes. One central reason for that is the lower capital gains tax rate. The highest rate of taxation for capital gains is 20 percent (for federal taxes), while the highest rate on annual income from work is 39.5 percent.

To better examine the issue, we can use the example professional sports. When fans read news about conflicts between a team's players and owners, they express frustration and disbelief about the "millionaires arguing with billionaires." That statement is true. However, when it comes to paying federal taxes, average Americans have a lot in common with the players. The star quarterback might get paid $10 million a year, but he pays twice the tax rate for his work than the owner pays for his capital gains. The quarterback pays 39.5 percent of his work income while the owner pays not more than 20 percent. So next time you watch the Super Bowl, just remember that the players on the field pay more in taxes, as a percentage of income, than the rich spectators in the high-priced private boxes.

Here is another example. Think about a woman (Beth) who falls into the top income bracket, making more the $450,000 a year. She earns that money doing actual work as a doctor, so she will pay an effective tax rate of about 39 percent before deductions. Compare Beth with another person, Alex, who makes $450,000 in capital gains income. He only pays 20 percent of that profit to the federal government. The system is designed to benefit people like Alex who make money from capital gains rather than people like Beth who work. In effect, the people like Alex benefit from a positive feedback loop.

To illustrate this point, assume that Beth takes no deductions or write-offs; therefore, she pays the full tax rate of 39.5 percent. In this case, she will pay about $178,000 in taxes and her after-tax income would be about $272,000. As for Alex, he also makes $450,000 in income, but the source is capital gains rather than work. Alex is not a chump. He knows how the financial system works. So, rather than drawing an annual salary, Alex plays the stock market, buying and selling assets, holding them for a year and then selling them. Because he keeps his gains under $518,000, his tax rate on that income will be 15 percent. As a result, Alex will pay $67,500 in federal taxes, which is less than half of what Beth paid. Alex's take home income for the year would be $382,500.

With those hypothetical examples in mind, we can look at what is happening in the real world. In fiscal year 2020, Americans reported $8.4 trillion in salaries and wages to the IRS, and they reported $1.1 trillion in capital gains. According to the Tax Policy Center, the richest 1 percent of Americans made about 79 percent of all US capital gains in 2019. Now consider this: The richest 0.1 percent gained *half* of that $1.1 trillion in capital gains income. So, the top 0.1 percent of American taxpayers, or about 120,000 households, made about $600 billion in capital gains in 2019. For comparison, the poorest one-fifth of American households, totaling about sixty-six million people, earned about $252 billion from salaries and wages in 2022, according to the US Census

Bureau. Take a moment to think about those stats. Sixty-six million Americans earned—through hard work—less than half of what the richest 120,000 made on capital gains in just one year.

Another way that the wealthy reduce their taxes with capital gains tax provisions is through stock buybacks. A stock buyback is a financial mechanism by which a company that issued stocks buys them back from investors. This practice might not seem so bad; after all, people buy and sell stocks all the time. But stock buybacks are different because stockholders sell the stocks back to the company rather than to other shareholders or new investors.

Until the 1980s, stock buybacks were illegal. Once they were legalized (thank Ronald Reagan and Congress for that), stock buybacks quickly became a staple tactic for concentrating wealth among the fewest people possible. Stock buybacks were previously illegal because they have a pernicious, two-fold effect. First, they almost always occur at the expense of average investors while benefiting institutional investors. In effect, they further concentrate the control of companies in the hands of the investor class, the people who already own most of a company's shares. Second, stock buybacks artificially drive up stock prices. This happens because the supply of shares goes down when the stock is in demand. If the institutional investors choose to sell their stocks later, they will almost certainly fetch a higher price, thus making the institutional investors richer. Here we find another way that the legal system since the 1980s foments income and wealth inequality.

Stock buybacks have a third nefarious effect: The company cannot use money from buybacks for reinvestments that would benefit the broader economy. No hiring new workers, no higher wages and salaries, no capital investment in new equipment, no expansion of the business, no new research and development. When that money leaves the company in the form of a stock buyback, the firm's board or managers can plausibly, albeit dishonestly, say that the company does not have the money to hire more staff, increase salaries, or make other investments. Companies may issue preferred or common stock, and the difference is what one would expect; common stocks receive dividends at the discretion of the board of directors, whereas preferred stocks receive dividends set at required rates. Guess which type of stock most people own?

In the recent case of a General Motors stock buyback, the company CFO, Paul Jacobson, said this: "Moving forward, we expect to continue returning excess capital to our shareholders and further reducing the share count."[21] The company announced this round of buybacks right after concluding a deal with the United Auto Workers union, saying that it would immediately buy back $6.8 billion of its common stock, with further buybacks of about $4 billion planned for 2024. Over the last ten years, the number of GM common shares decreased from 1.54 billion in 2015 to 1.15 billion at the end of fiscal year 2023. According to the company's 2024 SEC filings, the number of preferred shares remains at two billion.[22] This trend further concentrates the holding of stocks by institutional investors and wealthy individuals.[23] We are not singling out GM; rather, we want to illustrate one of the ways that our economy is rigged to concentrate wealth among a small group of wealthy individuals.

Another way stock buybacks encourage the concentration of wealth is related to a problem called the "disutility of illiquidity." This term is a fancy way for economists to say that holding assets, like stocks, favors those who can afford to keep holding them.

During a difficult time in life, average American investors might experience more pressure to liquidate an asset, which means they miss out on the future value of the asset after an economic or personal crisis. For example, suppose that our friends Jenny and Chad each received $100 worth of stock in Apple Computers in 1980. This stock went public in December 1980 at $22 per share, so they would have received 4.54 shares. If they both held on to that investment, their shares would be worth about $67,000 today. However, because Chad had a higher income during his career, he would have been better able to hold those shares through the ups and downs of the market. Jenny, however, had an absentee partner, two children, and low-wage jobs. During a personal crisis or broader economic downturn, she would be forced to look at that $100 dollar investment in Apple and think: *My family needs real apples; time to sell these pieces of paper.* Jenny's lack of cash on hand would almost certainly drive her to sell her shares. She would have to sell her stake in the larger American economy.

The income made from a stock buyback scheme almost always counts as capital gains, which, as we have seen, means that the income will not be taxed at a rate higher than 20 percent. Moreover, if the owner of the stock dies, her shares will pass directly to the inheritor without being taxed, further entrenching intergenerational wealth. The inheritor will only pay taxes on assets worth more than $13.6 million.

Who Pays Taxes?

Next, we need to dispel a myth related to who pays taxes. Various think tanks, including the Cato Institute, drawing on published IRS data, assert that the top 50 percent of households by income pay 97.7 percent of the total US tax revenue.[24] These numbers are based on the 158 million Americans who filed individual tax returns in 2021. The Cato Institute, using the 2021 IRS data, calculates that the bottom 50 percent of income earners make 10.4 percent of the nation's total "adjusted gross income" while paying only 2.3 percent of the total income taxes.

On the surface, this analysis creates the appearance that the wealthiest individuals are overburdened. However, those numbers mean that half the American population *only earns 10 percent* of the nation's total adjusted income each year! Please read that again. Half of all working Americans collectively earn, at most, 10 percent of all annual income in the United States. The top 1 percent takes home 26 percent of all income. Approximately three million wealthy people take home at least two-and-a-half times more income than roughly 165 million Americans combined.

Moreover, remember that "adjusted gross income" (AGI) includes income beyond the obvious categories like wages, salaries, business income, and capital gains. AGI includes all assistance payments from state and federal governments to low-income Americans. This includes, but is not limited to, Social Security payments to grandma, disability payments to those with serious medical problems, and federal insurance programs like Medicare and Medicaid. This has the effect of pumping up the incomes of the bottom half as a top line number. For accounting purposes, there are good reasons to do this, but it obscures the fact that a large percentage of US income derives from programs *into which citizens have already paid.* The AGI number serves to paper over the degree of income disparity in the US.

The Cato Institute often points to the dollar amounts paid by taxpayers without referring to the tax rate. Thus, their analysis assumes that the tax burden for someone making $30,000 a year is the same as the burden for someone making $3 million a year. It is true that, on average, a person in the bottom 50 percent who earns $30,000 a year will pay "only" 3.7 percent in federal income taxes, or about $1,100. However, the hardship this person will endure upon sending that amount to the IRS will be far more severe than the hardship of someone in the top 1 percent who earns $3.3 million and pays 26 percent to the IRS.

Paths for People

Before we offer our suggestions for dealing with the problems described in this chapter, please remember that we are not financial advisors. We encourage everyone to seek counsel from professionals. There are also many good books that offer financial advice and courses to improve financial literacy. Having stated that disclaimer, what can average Americans like us do?

Our first idea assumes that you have a bank or credit union that offers reasonable interest rates for money deposited in a savings account. Start by calculating how much your employer is withholding for state and federal taxes from each of your paychecks. Then ask your employer to stop withholding those income taxes from your paycheck. Put the amount that would have otherwise gone straight to the IRS into the savings account. Over the course of a year, that money will earn a little interest (current rates for a ten-month certificate of deposit are about 4 to 5 percent). At tax time, use the money in the savings account to pay your taxes, and pocket the interest. This trick will not make you rich, but it will generate a bit of extra income every April. The key is to make sure you do not use the money needed for taxes for some other purpose. The interest earned after you pay your taxes can be reinvested or used for an emergency.

Second, we can reduce the ongoing concentration of wealth held by big banks by using a local bank or credit union. The latter option is preferable because credit union depositors own the institution. Thus, if the credit union makes a decision that members dislike, the members can advocate for a reversal. This may or not work, but credit unions give members a little more leverage and control over their financial lives. You can be sure that the boards of big banks like Bank of America or Wells Fargo do not seriously consider customers' input. Every little bit of money that does not go to the big banks is a tiny degree of financial freedom for the rest of us.

Second, financial stability usually requires relational networks. A father who loses his job but has a supportive network of family and friends will be more resilient than a man who is isolated from the community. One way for Americans to strengthen relational connections is to join a mutual aid society. These organizations are exactly what the name suggests; groups of people who come together to help one another out. The Red Cross and the Salvation Army both began as mutual aid societies. (They became larger than what we have in mind.) Some mutual aid societies function within the context of a church, and some are secular. Some are limited to a single neighborhood, and others might operate across states and regions. The objectives of a mutual aid society are serious, but these organizations' meetings and events can also be socially fun. In an age of smart-phone saturation it can be refreshing to interact with genuine, community-minded people.

To save money, we also recommend that you reduce the time spent with phones, tablets, computers, and TVs. Anything with a screen will flood your mind with advertising. The ads will try to convince you to buy things you probably do not need and to pay for services that will not improve your life. Perhaps the most insidious aspect of advertising is its power to tell people what their lives "should" look like. Stepping away from this constant stream of materialist messaging can only improve mental health, as well as our bank accounts.

Another way to save money is to look for goods and services you have not used in the last six months. Then estimate how much money you spent over the last year on those unneeded things. That will enable you to see how much money you could save by cutting this stuff out of your life. Sell or give away the things you do not need. Once you do that, cut future expenses on unnecessary products and services. Hopefully, this process will help you think about what you really value. Some people reading this book might not have any fat in their budget to cut. If so, please disregard the budgeting portion of this pathway.

Paths for Policy

We believe that policymakers should implement an idea proposed by Milton and Rose Friedman in their book *Capitalism and Freedom*. This might seem to contradict our main arguments because Milton Friedman, a Nobel Prize-winning economist, pushed for libertarian policies that increased inequality in the US. However, we agree with his "negative income tax" (NIT) proposal. The basic concept is that employed workers who fall beneath a particular income level should receive a simple, no-strings-attached cash transfer from the government. He argued that this would offer economic benefits to society and to workers. Providing cash would give workers freedom to use the money according to their specific needs. By contrast, food stamps can only be used for food, but not medicine or clothes. The amount offered could be based on a simple assessment of each recipient's taxable income. This approach would be better than typical welfare programs that require applicants to answer extensive lists of questions and meet numerous requirements. As a result, more poor households would be included in the program.

This policy should be applied to all people regardless of employment status. If the benefit is only offered to people who are formally employed, it will face the same fatal poison as employer-sponsored health insurance, which leaves unemployed or self-employed people without health care. The loss of health care makes it harder for injured or sick people to work, which in turn undermines their ability to be self-sufficient. If government relief benefits had been conditioned on formal employment during the Great Depression, millions more people would have starved. Likewise, if temporary relief measures during the Great Recession and the Covid-19 pandemic had been tied to formal employment, many more Americans would have fallen into potentially permanent poverty traps. The existence of the Earned Income Tax Credit is necessary to reduce inequality, but it is not sufficient because many people do not have formal employment. Economist Hernando de Soto Polar, in his books *The Mystery of Capital* and *The Other Path*, writes extensively about how to improve conditions for people with informal jobs.

The most significant potential tool for combating inequality in our lifetimes is the Universal Basic Income (UBI). If lawmakers and policymakers are serious about reducing inequality, they should focus on implementing a UBI. A UBI further simplifies the Friedmans' NIT proposal by removing the requirement to be formally employed. A UBI removes the final vestige of corporate influence over efforts to reduce inequality, and it would provide a foundation for the most vulnerable populations to escape poverty traps. Some critics of the idea argue that a UBI system would increase identity fraud and that it would incentivize "welfare queens" to take advantage of a lax and overly generous system. These arguments are worth considering, but we believe UBI costs would be lower than the costs of corporate fraud, tax evasion, unfair tax rates, stock buybacks, and all the other ways that wealthy people and large corporations benefit from our rigged system.

According to the US Census and the Federal Reserve, the estimated percentage of individuals in poverty in the United States in 2022 was 12.6 percent. Roughly one of every ten Americans lives below an arbitrarily low poverty line of $15,000 per year. How much would it cost per year to pay these people a UBI of $1000 a month with no strings attached? If 39.6 million Americans received $12,000 per year, the UBI program would cost roughly $475 billion per year. Compare that amount to the $600 billion that the top one-tenth of the top 1 percent of Americans made in capital gains income in 2020. And remember that most of those people only paid 15 percent in taxes on that income. Who is really benefitting from "welfare"?

CHAPTER 5

Hit the Books, Dummy!

The way to get ahead in the world is with a sound education. If you plan to go into the trades, you will need to know what an ohm is and why you should measure it, unless you want to get electrocuted. In the first chapter, we saw that Marty went to trade school and managed to claw his way into the middle class. Meanwhile Jenny, lacking stable housing and reliable pay, never could afford tuition for any additional schooling, so she always had to make do with low-paying jobs.

In recent decades, most parents have assumed that sending their kids to a four-year college would set them up for lifelong economic stability. This assumption was based on the experience of those who came of age in the 1970s. That was certainly the case for the authors of this book. When we were young, our parents taught us the importance of getting a four-year degree. When it came time for high school graduation, we both dutifully packed up and headed off to a state-sponsored university. One of us briefly considered taking a post-high school gap year to work and figure out what he wanted to do in life.

Unbeknownst to the younger version of ourselves, we started our university paths at just the right time. Thanks to policies that originated during the Civil War, Kansas and Oklahoma had quality universities that were, in 2001, relatively affordable. But within a decade, only students from wealthy families had the possibility of graduating from college without significant student loan debt.

Today the cost of a four-year degree has ballooned. Some people question whether the returns on that investment will be worthwhile. At the time of this writing, federally backed student loan debt is a whopping $1.4 trillion. The average borrower has nearly $40,000 in debt. Those numbers do not include private loans, which have been estimated to be an additional $150 billion to $200 billion. Lower-income students, because they have less support from family, often feel compelled to take on more debt to obtain a degree.

The levels of student loan debt have skyrocketed even though some researchers believe there is a lower demand for some degrees. From a basic economics perspective, the supply of graduates with two- and four-year degrees has steadily increased for decades, but the demand for some types of degrees has either leveled off or declined. So, depending on the field of study, the value of a diploma might be lower than in previous decades.

These trends have played out while financial pressures on universities have pushed them to accept money from private donors and foundations. In many cases, these private interests have been more interested in pushing their private agendas than supporting quality education. In the field of economics, for example, a small number of deep-pocketed donors operate through charitable foundations that fund pro-business think tanks on campus. Many of these think tanks pointedly ignore research about the shortcomings of the overall US economic model. With education budgets routinely reduced by state legislatures, universities are increasingly compelled to accept private money. Everyone knows that the university is essentially selling its name and credibility in return for private funding. The pressure has been similar at private universities and colleges.

Sending Up Flares in the Night

Any undergraduate, and hopefully some high school graduates, can recite Plato's Allegory of the Cave. Even if overused, it is a useful depiction of how our perceptions of reality may be nothing more than shadows on a cave wall. Plato concluded the allegory by suggesting that philosophy is the one tried and true method of crawling past the shadows of the cave and into the daylight, the realm of "true knowledge." The allegory implies that we need to carefully examine our beliefs.

In the social sciences, including economics and history, there are precious few laboratories in which we can repeat experiments in controlled environments and then compare the results. That means that millions of people strive daily to make economic decisions in a complex, information-inundated society without any real certainty. It can be hard to hire an employee, find a doctor, or buy a car. Life can feel like we are in Plato's cave.

A better metaphor would be a cloudy night on a rural road: no stars to guide you, the moon visible only through fleeting breaks in the clouds, no street lights, no people—just tall corn as high as an elephant's eye. In a stroke of good luck, you see a bright flare above the cornfield. The red light illuminates everything within a hundred yards. You rush toward the source of the flare hoping to find the person who shot it into the sky.

In modern societies, our most-trusted "flares" within any given "cornfield" of life are those with a university degree. People who do not have a university degree can be sources of illumination, but we long ago agreed (thankfully) that doctors, engineers, architects, and other professionals should have more than a few hours of YouTube instruction. We believe that to be good at something, people need to learn by studying, often for years. And the proof of that learning is often a diploma from an accredited, degree-granting institution. That had been the trusted standard for decades.

However, there has always been another side to this narrative. Many people think that a diploma represents status more than merit. Increasing numbers of people believe that degrees are "signals" of a person's worldview or character; that is, the ability to persevere through four years of college. As a result, many question the economic value of college degrees. They believe that spending four years in college can lead to a quagmire of debt without a good financial return. The students who are most likely to be trapped by debt with no way to climb the socioeconomic ladder are those who can least afford a degree. The US has the most respected institutions of higher education in the world. So, how did we get here?

In 1920, roughly 4 percent of Americans age twenty-three and older had a bachelor's degree or higher. Barely 25 percent of the population had a high school diploma. According to the US Census Bureau, the average number of years of completed education at that time was 8.2. A lot has changed since then. Today 37 percent of Americans have a post-secondary degree and about 90 percent of the population has at least a high school diploma (or equivalent). The average years of educational attainment is 16.3. These numbers reflect a major push during the twentieth century to build more schools and to compel more young people to attend them. Americans are smarter, or at least better educated.

However, in terms of economic outcomes, what benefits have resulted from all that schooling? The correlation between more education and greater lifetime income still exists. By some measures, including those from the Bureau of Labor Statistics, those with a doctoral degree earn, on average, three-and-a-half times more than a person with less than a high school diploma. People with a bachelor's degree earn almost twice as much as a person with only a high school diploma. People with post-high school degrees also gain access to more interesting career opportunities, and they are less likely to lose their jobs in a recession. So, even if people do not care about the intangible value of a college education (e.g., broader understanding of the world, critical thinking skills, relationships), we can at least appreciate the utilitarian argument that getting that extra piece of paper will lead to a better-paying job.

Unfortunately, those statistics obscure a trend that began right around 1999. According to the Bureau of Labor Statistics, the ratio of unemployed people with less than a high school diploma compared to those with advanced degrees began to even out. In 1999, for every unemployed person with at least a bachelor's degree there were about four unemployed people with less than a high school diploma, a 1 to 4 ratio. In 2023, that ratio had narrowed to 1 to 2.5, meaning that for every unemployed person with at least a bachelor's degree there were about 2.5 unemployed people without a high school diploma.

What this data means is that a higher degree still provides people with more job security, but not as much as it did in the late 1990s. College-educated workers look more like every other worker when it comes to employment, wages, and overall employability. Obviously, the area of study each student chooses has a significant influence on job security and wages. According to the American Academy of Arts and Sciences, the biggest jumps by field of study between 1980 and 2020 occurred in health sciences and engineering, fields from which we might expect high levels of employment.[25] The percentage of people pursuing degrees in the humanities has declined. Even though more people have pursued in-demand degrees like engineering, the overall trend is that a higher degree provides less job security than it did in the late 1990s. Today, for every unemployed person with at least one framed college diploma hanging on the wall there are 2.5 unemployed dropouts. Thirty years ago, that ratio would have been 1 to 4.

This trend has occurred while the average wage-to-GDP gap has continued to widen, as described in chapter 2. This also suggests that advanced degrees do not pay as well as they used to. Everyone from doctors and lawyers to janitors and ditch diggers are seeing their wages shrink while the economy, measured on a macro level, continues to grow. To be clear, *everyone* is experiencing a decline in real wages. A dollar does not go as far as it used to, and neither does an advanced degree.

All these challenges present intractable problems. But that is not all. The relentless attacks on universities as bastions of "liberalism" and "elitism" further complicate the perceived value of a university education. The partisan attacks against universities place public discourse in a straitjacket. Students and professors must make a binary choice between wearing the "liberal" shirt or the "conservative" shirt. If you want to keep your job as a professor, or if you want to be taken seriously in public discourse, or if you want a prestigious university to stand behind your research, the professors and students must choose a shirt. This straitjacketing keeps the academics in one of two lines: red or blue, liberal or conservative, right or left. When the public sees the squabbling along partisan lines, people begin to distrust the long and amazing role of universities to provide well-researched knowledge about medicine, law, technology, agriculture, literature, civics, and engineering.

The Relational Value of College Education

Even if the average financial returns of a four-year degree are diminishing, one could argue that networking opportunities and connections to internships still make going to college worthwhile. This is a valid point. The formalized relationships between universities and potential employers offer easy enticement. But this argument misses the forest for the trees. Yes, the pipeline from college to employment does exist, but stratification between elite universities and good universities reinforces society's inequalities.

It should come as no surprise that affordability and access to the higher-tier schools filters out many first-generation and low-income applicants. The reasons for this vary as widely as the students themselves. For some, the eyewatering sticker prices of elite and flagship universities turn away many. For others, the lack of solid college-prep courses in high school is the limiting factor. Many children whose families are in the lower 40 percent by income do not know anyone close to them who went to college, and those kids are more likely to face challenges to health and welfare than their middle- and upper-class peers.

This sort of stratification has always been present in American society. But the situation today is distinct compared to previous generations. In the wake of World War II, the cost to attend a four year university plummeted because Americans made the collective choice to adequately fund the education system from top to bottom. Indeed, the three most affordable decades to attend a US university came between 1960 and 1990. In the intervening thirty or so years, the cost of attending even a state-sponsored school rose dramatically. We will focus more on monetary costs later in the chapter.

People tend to network within their socioeconomic class. They usually marry within their class as well. This potential barrier to family formation poses a challenge to the social health of America. People are drifting apart based on class and college affordability, and there is a rapidly opening rift between genders that threatens to create a new fault line in the fissures of our society. As of 2023, the data about who chooses to attend college revealed a disconcerting snapshot of future dating and marriage pools; specifically, 60 percent of entering first-year students were women and 40 percent were men.

What does this mean for the future stability of marriage and family? It is possible that women could expect to earn significantly more than men. This is not a bad thing; women have long earned less than men for the same work, and they should be properly compensated for their college degrees. However, problems within a marriage can emerge when one partner earns significantly more than the other, regardless of which partner earns more. It is also possible that overall downward mobility in the US could lead to the long-term impoverishment of America's middle and working classes—a great equalizer between men and women. Hooray.

The education gap may pose another challenge to forming families. Those with four-year degrees often maintain different interests than their high school and technical school counterparts. This also is not a bad thing; however, romantic relationships between people with starkly different educational backgrounds often leave the less-educated partner feeling insecure or inferior. This strain, added to other daily stresses, can easily break a relationship or even a family. People within educational classes often have trouble making time for each other, romantically or otherwise. Now add gender and economic differences into that mix and we can see the potential for long-term barriers to establishing families.

The Economics of University Consolidation

Universities, like any modern institution (or firm), seek to reduce costs and maximize profit. A firm that produces a good or service with "increasing returns to scale" will see its costs of production fall as it produces more of the product. The more Amazon sells, the cheaper it is for Amazon to produce more. Similarly, as universities produce more graduates who enter the workforce, they can receive more from donating alumni and subsidized enrollment. This lowers the operations costs over time. Thus, university systems experience the pressure to surrender to monopoly forces, either by eliminating smaller, regional colleges or by buying them.

For example, vast educational systems like the University of California, the University of Texas, Texas A&M, and the University of Minnesota agglomerate smaller regional schools underneath their bureaucratic umbrellas. Regional accreditation boards reinforce the monopolization of big university systems by punishing schools that cannot afford the reaccreditation process required by their respective systems (e.g., the AACSB system and the SACS-COC system for business schools). Regional branches like West Texas A&M University, the University of California in Merced, and the University of Texas in Dallas allow for a much larger scale of student-loan-subsidized enrollment, which feeds the operations of the school and increases the likelihood that the school will produce donating alumni. High-level sports teams also generate large sums of money for major university systems, which marginalizes smaller colleges and reinforces the monopolization trends. Small schools are increasingly being absorbed into larger university systems. These market trends have little to do with the quality of education or graduates' preparedness for serving the real-world needs of companies.

It should be evident at this point that education will not save us from the wave of inequality. Education is strongly influenced by the same monopolistic pressures that finance and technology sectors experience, and those pressures drive inequality. Students often feel pressured to take on tens of thousands of dollars of debt, but the diplomas increasingly do not provide adequate financial returns.

Diploma Mills or Money Launderers?

Protests on college campuses have attempted to compel universities to "divest" their endowments of investments in corporations deemed to be unethical, such as those that produce weapons. Students or faculty members make appeals to boards of trustees or major donors who may, under pressure, cut funding to the university. Donors usually disregard these appeals because they receive a tax write-off for the full value of their donations. Some states offer tax credits as well. Large donations often eliminate the donor's need to pay federal income taxes in a given year. The donors might also receive an in-kind return from the university. In other words, the financial incentives for individual wealthy donors who give to universities are immense. Donors usually do not care much about the academic achievement within a university; they mostly enjoy being associated with a big-name school, and they like the financial benefits. So, donors are not easily compelled to pull money from an endowment for political or academic purposes. This sets up an interesting incentive structure for universities. Aside from the long-term need to maintain accreditation, the schools are incentivized to please donors who will hopefully write a large check. This goal could be contrary to the stated mission of a university as a center for independent and creative research, education, and mentorship. The pursuit of donors could entice universities to inflate students' grades to maintain stable enrollment and retention rates, which play a role in fundraising efforts. Those rates are reported to the donors, accrediting institutions, and state legislatures. This does not mean that all universities comply with the demands of donors; nevertheless, the financial incentives are prominent, and they are often disconnected from the educational and financial needs of students.

Interest Never Sleeps

From the end of World War II to the early 1990s, investing in a college education proved to be a good bet for American families. What about today? Is a university education a sound economic choice? To best answer this question, we need to look at the math and talk about compound interest.

As of 2023, the student loan debt in the US was $1.4 trillion (not including privately held debt). Approximately 43.2 million people carry a heavy burden of federal student loan debt, with an average balance of $37,000. Student loan debt as a percentage of GDP was about 6.6 percent, enough to cause a modest drag on the economy. For these indebted Americans, the problem is more tangible. An unsubsidized loan with a principal of $10,000 and an interest rate of 6.8 percent, adds up to $1.68 each day. The loan will continue to accrue debt even if it is in deferment. That amount will be added to the principal of the loan when the deferment period ends. Because borrowers are disproportionately from lower-income families, student loan debt compounds inequality. Furthermore, first generation or minority college students are less likely to be informed of the risks of prolonging their loan repayments. Some scholarship and financial aid offices are more interested in pairing students with loans—because the money will go to the college—than they are in providing financial education and debt counseling to students and families.

The average per-month student loan payment in 2023 was $500 per month for an undergraduate degree. That monthly payment increased to between $500 and $900 for a master's degree.

People with doctoral degrees paid at least $900 per month in 2023. The average borrower takes twenty years to pay back a student loan debt.

What does this mean on a paycheck-to-paycheck basis? For someone with an associate's degree, the average take-home pay is $4,000 month. For those with a bachelor's degree, the average take-home pay is $6,000 per month. This means that the average student loan payment is 12 percent of monthly income. That percentage drops slightly to 10 percent for those with advanced degrees, but the result is functionally the same. Add a 12 percent loan to the overall cost of living and it is easy to see how student loan debt will place burdens on the borrower, place a drag on the overall economy, and worsen inequality.

Paths for People

Where should a young person get an education? No economic decision occurs in a vacuum. Families and students might have many nonfinancial reasons for going to college; however, we will present some ideas that pertain to the economic costs and benefits of preparing for professional life.

Consider Non-College Alternatives

We need to think about the relationships between education and the job market. In other words, we need to ask what employers will be willing to pay for in the years ahead. Some trade groups claim that the US will add about 1.6 million blue collar jobs over the next five years. They also state that there are about four hundred thousand blue collar positions open right now. And those numbers only reflect the *companies* that are hiring or plan to hire. Data from trade organizations are not always exact, but the overall national need is clear. There should be a demand for those types of services now and in the future.

We all know what happens to wages when there is a strong demand and a weak supply: wages *should* rise. But do they? Maybe. There are many factors that can affect labor supply and demand, and there are many factors that can affect wages. Who would have expected the impact of the Covid-19 pandemic on the global economy? Who could have foretold Russia's invasion of Ukraine? Who would have imagined that Donald Trump would disrupt the world's economy in early 2025 with on-and-off tariffs?

Despite life's uncertainties, it seems clear that gaining an education that equips people for high-level trades is a sound bet. This does not mean that a four-year degree is not economically worthwhile, but it does mean that there are good opportunities for young professionals who want an alternative to a college degree. And this type of education usually costs much less than a four-year degree, which therefore reduces the debt burden.

Trade Schools, Community Colleges, and Post-Graduate Degrees

There are still a couple of bright spots for those who want to pursue an affordable education without drowning in debt. In a great many places around the United States, community colleges and trade schools are great options.

Trade schools increasingly offer a wide array of professional pathways designed to meet the needs of the labor market. Beyond the more common career paths (e.g., plumber, electrician, nursing, etc.), other options include aviation, shipbuilding, furniture making, master brewing, and even international coffee grading (cupping). These courses usually take one or two years and offer direct links to apprenticeships and internships.

Community colleges offer a range of two-year degrees. People who want to pursue a four-year degree can save a lot of money by completing their basic education courses (the first two years of a four-year degree) at a community college and then transfer their credits to a four-year college or university. Many states also give students the opportunity to graduate from high school with an associate's degree. The students finish their last two years of high school at a nearby community college, attending for free. When they graduate, they only need to pay for two more years to earn a bachelor's degree. That option saves two years of time and reduces overall college costs by half.

Finally, many high school seniors think they should earn a bachelor's degree at an elite school. However, for the reasons described earlier in the chapter, a four-year degree often does not mean as much as it did in the past, at least in terms of financial returns. Therefore, we suggest that people who want a bachelor's degree should study at a good public university where they can pay in-state tuition. They usually should not pursue a bachelor's degree from an expensive private university or college. At the state university, students should do everything possible to get high grades, get involved in professional societies, and take advantage of university-linked internships. Upon completing their four-year degrees, they can then think about pursuing a post-graduate degree at a more expensive school. By keeping costs low during the undergraduate years, students will have more ability to invest in post-graduate degrees.

The Debt Calculator

Speaking of student loan debt, we stress the importance of avoiding it—or at least keeping it to a minimum. We do not mean to impose a fixed rule that covers all situations. Those who want to become a doctor will usually incur a large debt to pay for medical school, but because doctors' salaries are typically high, the debt burden will be easier for them to carry. By contrast, a student should not take out large loans to get an English degree. In this milieu of tough questions and degree variables, how much debt is too much? In other words, what is the maximum amount of debt one should assume to pay for an education?

This turns out to be a double-layered question. First, imagine that a young woman (Wendy) is trying to decide whether to go to college, purely from an economic perspective. First, she needs to consider how long the education will take (e.g., four years). Then she needs to estimate her out-of-pocket tuition costs during those years. (Colleges usually provide a cost calculator on their websites.) She might assume that her real tuition costs will be $15,000 per year, or $60,000 total. The next step for Wendy is to estimate how much she might earn during four years in a full-time job, assuming she chooses not to attend college. She thinks that she could earn $40,000 per year working as a medical receptionist, which over four years would generate $160,000. Then she needs to add that amount to the expected cost of tuition. So, her total real cost of choosing to attend college for four years would be about $220,000. This number, which does not yet include the cost of interest on student loans, can then be compared with the potential salary she is likely to earn with a degree.

Many factors can affect the results of this comparison. For example, Wendy might work a part-time job while she is in school. Other factors might include the cost of living, student loan interest rates, and the long-term viability of the degree. But this baseline number can enable her to discern how much debt she should incur.

Wendy assumes she can cover her room and board and basic expenses by working part-time while she takes classes. So, she will only need to find money to cover the $60,000 for tuition. Her family is not able to help. She might be able to get some scholarships beyond the normal state and federal grants, but to be conservative, she assumes that she will need a total loan amount of not more than $60,000 over four years. With those caveats in mind, Wendy can use a paycheck calculator to figure out how much debt she should or should not take on. We encourage readers to use the calculator. It can be found at the end of the book in the endnotes section.[26]

Wendy assumes that she will pay 6 percent interest on the $60,000 loan principal. She would like to pay that off in no more than twenty years. After doing careful research about her expected earnings with a degree in computer science, she is reasonably sure that she can land a job with a starting salary of $80,000 per year. The calculator tells her that her monthly payment will be about $430 per month. It also tells her that she will need to earn at least $64,500 per year to comfortably pay that monthly bill, assuming she incurs no other debts. Based on these numbers, Wendy concludes that her plan is relatively safe.

There is another way of looking at Wendy's situation. If Wendy does in fact pay $430 per month for twenty years on her $60,000 loan, at a fixed 6 percent interest rate, she will pay a total of $43,000 in total interest. So, her total cost for the four-year degree (tuition plus interest) will be $103,000. She can add that number to the money she would have earned by working a full-time job rather than going to school, which, as we saw above, was $160,000. So, the total cost of the four-year degree would be about $263,000.

If Wendy does in fact earn $80,000 per year, she would need about three and a half years to break even. After four years in the job, she would be making a profit. Moreover, her earning potential after four years of work would probably go up, assuming she is a good employee. By comparison, if she did not go to college and earned $50,000 per year as a medical receptionist, her long-term earning potential would be about 50 percent less than what she could earn with a degree.

Wendy's circumstances are conservative and reasonable, but they are also not guaranteed. Many students graduate with similar debt levels, but they struggle to find work that pays enough to reduce their monthly debt burdens. Quite a few young men and women have fallen into debt traps in recent decades. As the cost of an education spiraled upward since the 1990s, more people have been squeezed out of middle-class stability. Debt peonage stifles economic freedom. So, it is crucial to keep debt as low as possible.

Paths for Policy

For at least a century, state universities have been places to find leafy and placid campuses, the irrational exuberance of youth, and the willingness to consider new and unusual ideas. State universities have changed a lot since the 1970s and 1980s, when Baby Boomers left their wild college parties to engage in a mature world. The cost of tuition and fees, textbooks, housing, and food has increased exponentially during the past forty years.

The reason for the rising cost of education is simple: financial support for state universities has collapsed. It is that simple. Look up any data you like about this topic: state spending per student, state spending per capita, student debt levels after graduation, the cost of tuition adjusted for inflation, fees as a percentage of total cost. Every single metric shows a drop in state spending and a rise in costs for students. This trend took off in the wake of the 2008 Great Recession, which cratered state budgets. When the budgets needed to be cut, policymakers typically found it convenient to apply the knife on the necks of institutions that could jack up their prices to cover the shortfall. This happened in state capitals across the country from 2009 to 2011. State lawmakers decided to cut spending on higher education to help cover budget deficits, but they also did not restore that funding when the budgetary situation stabilized.

There is a more insidious side to the story. For every budget crisis forced on a state by macroeconomic factors beyond the control of lawmakers and governors, state-level leaders often manufacture their own budget shortfalls. One way they do this by returning tax revenue to citizens rather than misspending it themselves. States also provide large tax breaks to the biggest businesses and to people in the highest income brackets. (What a surprise!) Never mind that every tax dollar not collected from those who are most able to afford it is a dollar not invested in educating future generations, the young people who go into debt to study at state colleges and universities.

It is time for state representatives and governors to change their thinking on state education funding priorities. Our point here is not subtle: If states are truly the laboratories of democracy, then it is time for state lawmakers to learn from the recent past and redesign the experiment in ways that reduce long-term inequality outcomes. For over forty years, the federal government and the states have been relying on neoliberal policies designed to favor the wealthiest sectors of society. The current rules have produced a form of socialism for the wealthy and powerful. The systemic changes required to shift funding to those who need it, and to shift more of the tax burden to those who can most afford it can, in fact, start at the state level.

CHAPTER 6

Technology Will Save Us!

What is technology? Is it strictly defined by iPhones, steam engines, and other labor-saving devices? Is a rock a type of technology? We would define technology as any tool made by humans to amplify their own innate abilities and/or save labor while performing a task.

In the field of economics, technology affects the labor market in two principal ways: factor augmenting and task substitution. *Factor augmenting* serves to increase worker productivity across all tasks. A factory worker can complete tasks faster and better with a pneumatic wrench than she can with a hand-turned wrench, at least for some jobs. A file clerk can accomplish more work in less time by using a computer than he could with a paper and pen. *Task substitution* occurs when a machine replaces the human worker so that the human can focus on other tasks. Robots on an assembly line are examples of task substitution. The jury is still out, but artificial intelligence could be used for factor augmenting and/ or task substitution in the service economy rather than in the manufacturing sector.

Many people believe that new technologies always solve problems. When inequality occurs because of technology, a common defense is that technological progress is a stepping stone toward better ways of living. Technologists argue that new technologies will benefit society overall, even if it means they will make certain jobs redundant. The proverbial rising tide lifts all boats.

During the nineteenth century and the first half of the twentieth century, the belief that technology would provide better ways to make more stuff available, thus improving the population's material situation, proved to be mostly true. Some trades went away, but people now have more hats and cheaper barrels. So, in a broad sense, the loss of hat- and barrel-making jobs may have been a worthwhile sacrifice. Labor-saving devices have made numerous professions easier and more efficient. Economist Robert Solow won a Nobel Prize for his research on this topic. He found that a nation can escape stagnant growth by increasing the use of technology as a factor of production. Overreliance on physical capital, or labor, leads to choke points that cause diminishing marginal returns. Solow's work was revolutionary for its deep insight into how output, specifically GDP, can be boosted by technological advances that contribute to a nation's production capacity. However, Solow's model does not include any conclusions about inequality.

Economist Simon Kuznets posited (incorrectly with his abuse of cross sectional versus time series methods) that inequality rises and then falls as a country goes from low-income GDP to middle-income GDP and then to high-income GDP. There is no rigorous economic evidence that an increase in output—driven by technology or otherwise—will automatically lead to a decrease in inequality.

In short, technology can increase productivity and GDP, but it is an overreach to say that more tech will always lead to a bigger, better economy with a higher standard of living *for everyone*. The argument that more technology will even out any wealth and income imbalances is overly optimistic. In fact, technology often increases inequality. It is true that technology can help workers become more productive and help consumer goods become more widely available, but to where do the profits flow? What are the costs to the American worker?

As we showed earlier in the book, productivity and compensation increased at basically the same rates between 1948 and 1978. Labor-saving devices and complex technologies did indeed lift all boats. Then, in the early 1980s, that trend decoupled; GDP increased but wages stagnated, falling increasingly behind. Today, Americans are more productive than ever, but their compensation is barely 10 percent better than their peers in the 1970s.[27] (See figure 2-4 for a visual representation.)

Why did the US experience this "great decoupling"? The answer is not simple. For starters, the upward trajectory of technological growth and sophistication may have plateaued; that is, the proverbial rising tide stopped lifting all boats in the early 1980s. In addition, there is ample evidence that the consumption of fossil fuels and population growth during the post-war baby boom caused economic growth more than new technologies.

Data from the Bureau of Labor Statistics and the Economic Policy Institute show that between the first quarter of 1948 and the first quarter of 2024, productivity increased by 393 percent. Unfortunately, during that same period, compensation only increased by 240 percent (see figure 2-4). By applying logarithmic methods to the data, we find additional mathematical evidence that productivity increases have not equally benefited average American workers. To whatever degree technology has been jumpstarting output and productivity, it is not doing the same for worker compensation. The tide is rising, but the boats are drydocked or sinking. American workers have created a lot of value, but they have not been fairly compensated for all that work.

Does Technology Drive Growth and Reduce Inequality?

For a long time, many economists answered that question in the affirmative. End of story. Next topic. Earlier in the chapter, we mentioned Nobel Prize-winning economist Robert Solow. The Solow-Swan model, articulated in the 1950s, sought to explain long-run economic growth through the accumulation of capital, fixed labor inputs, and increased productivity due to technological innovation. In effect, the model showed that technological innovation could explain, at least in part, continued economic growth because innovation helps a country avoid the law of diminishing returns.

To explain all this in simpler terms, imagine that you run a mill that turns cotton into bolts of cloth. If technology does not change, then you will continue to use the same loom year after year. The only reason to buy a new one would be if the old one breaks and cannot be fixed. If you decide to buy a second loom, you might have to expand the mill to accommodate it and the extra workers. Those costs may not be worth it; the costs could outweigh whatever profits can be made. However, if someone invents a new type of loom that can double the amount of cloth your mill can spin, then you will not need to hire more workers or expand the mill. In this case, it makes sense to buy a new loom. This is an example of how technology can "avoid the law of diminishing returns" on capital investments (the building and the loom) and labor costs.

Until about the time when Solow received his Nobel Prize in 1987, this model painted a fairly accurate picture of the economy. Then, in 1992, economists Gregory Mankiw, David Romer, and David Weil modified the model with a critique. They pointed out that technology is *endogenous,* a word they used to say that technology depends as much on human capital as investment capital.

To explain their critique, imagine that you want to invest in a new loom for the mill, but none of your people know how to use it. Would this stop you from investing in it? The answer probably depends on the context. If the loom is just a more energy-efficient retread of an existing model, then you would probably invest in it. But if the new loom requires someone to know computer programing to operate the machine within tight parameters, that necessity might prevent you from investing in it. You would question whether half your workers need to learn computer programming to make it work and to synchronize it with the other machines in the mill. Do you really want to train three or more employees in computer programming? If they learn this new skill, will they want to keep working at your mill? This example shows that technology, on its own, does not necessarily drive improvements in productivity.

What about reductions in inequality? As described in chapter 2, the gap between GDP and income—the increase of inequality—began to increase in the 1980s and then expand in the 1990s. That was the same time that computing technology started to become ubiquitous. Did computers cause the change? Obviously, correlation does not equal causation. There were other factors behind "the great decoupling." In the 1990s, the pace of factory closures and the offshoring of white collar jobs, which started in the 1980s, picked up pace. Congress lowered corporate and top marginal tax rates, and former President Bill Clinton signed off on the repeal of the Glass-Stegall Act, which fueled bank consolidation. In short, many factors came together to decouple GDP from average wages.

However, information technology did enable each of these factors to move faster, shaking up more industries. Automation rendered many blue collar jobs redundant. Global telecommunications allowed call centers and back office work to take place wherever cheap labor and minimal infrastructure coincided. Computers transformed the stock market and investment banking from a messy, face-to-face affair to one dominated by digital spreadsheets and high-frequency trading. In other words, the biggest technological innovations since the 1960s put a lot of people out of work, in part by enabling American companies to ship jobs to people who would work for less pay. Policies either permitted or encouraged these changes, driving down employment while driving up corporate profits.

From 1953 to 1991, the gap between per-capita GDP and real income was expanding at a gradual rate. Economic inequality was not wildly out of control during those years. But starting in 1991, the gap between GDP and real income widened dramatically. That trend began with the 1990s tech boom and continued with the proliferation of computing into every facet of modern life.

Again, correlation is not the same as causation. Many factors have influenced the rise of inequality in the US. But we know that computing technology has increased economic growth, and we know from the data that information technology has not lifted all boats. If anything, information technology can be seen as one of inequality's apocalyptic horsemen. Computer technology has either shifted American jobs overseas or extracted more productivity from them at home. Regardless, American workers have seen nothing but wage stagnation for decades.

Computing technology has brought mindboggling benefits to every industry. Many innovations have saved lives. We are living in a special era. And yet, advances in information technology also have negative economic impacts. The computing power that allows researchers to collaborate across continents also allows capital to flow freely away from American workers. The easy movement of capital from one place to another should be a good thing; in theory, it should allow people to invest in business ventures in untapped markets. Unfortunately, a lot of capital has flowed freely to hidden accounts in offshore tax havens. Global Financial Integrity (GFI), an independent anticorruption watchdog, reports that more than seventy states or countries are home to "millions of hidden accounts, secret trusts, and anonymous corporations that allow individuals to hide their wealth and avoid taxes." GFI estimates that this system holds more than $50 trillion.[28]

No one enjoys paying taxes, but access to tax havens and shady bank accounts—facilitated by information technology—allows the top 1 percent to reduce their tax bills by siphoning vast amounts of money away from American workers. That means less money to reduce deficits, invest in infrastructure, or boost wages in education. The offshore concentration of wealth shifts the tax burden from the rich to everyone else.

Moreover, all the capital sitting in those accounts is never invested back into the broader economy. This lack of reinvestment has real-world impacts. If investing and consumption are the main drivers of our economy, then the secreting away of untold riches into shell companies reduces the macroeconomic multiplier effect of capital. At least since the 1980s, neoliberal politicians have been promising that lower taxes would "trickle down" to mainstream Americans. They said that businesses and corporations would have more money to reinvest in the economy, thereby creating new jobs and higher wages. After forty years of this experiment, there is no evidence this policy has worked, as reported by renowned economist Alan Blinder in his sweeping history of the US monetary system since 1961.[29] The reality, however, is that wealthy investors and corporations often park the money in offshore accounts. At the risk of being too blunt, those who preach trickle-down economics are pissing on us and telling us it is raining.

The money held offshore by the rich could be reinvested or taxed fairly, bringing broader benefits to the average Americans whose work generated the wealth in the first place. GDP could be growing at a higher rate. Capital could be used to invest more in science and technology, which is known to be a leading driver of long-term productivity and human well-being. We could reduce deficits and, therefore, the national debt, which would ease the tax burden on future generations. However, unless the underlying rules of the economy change, only those who hold the increasing returns of production will benefit. The rest of us will be left behind.

History shows us that the mantra "technology will save us" is not automatically true. Technology can play a significant role in improving the economy of a nation, but the broader outcomes for all citizens depend on how leaders implement technologies and how the profits are used. In other words, the policies and laws must be designed to benefit all of society, not just the elite.

Evidence for this point can be seen by comparing the relationship between inequality and rates of ownership of basic goods that were invented in the twentieth century: refrigerators, laundry machines, stoves and ovens, TVs, and cars. We can look first at washing machines and refrigerators because all people, regardless of class, need them. They will spend money on them no matter what. Then, if we compare the ownership rates of people in the top 10 percent with the ownership rates of people in the bottom 10 percent, we see strong ownership equality for these types of items.[30]

However, another barometer shows increasing inequality: the all-American automobile. What product could better symbolize the American value of freedom and the conquest of open spaces? And what better object to serve as a case study of compounding inequality? Some people argue that the widespread growth of car sales indicates a reduction in inequality. The data, however, shows a different story. Unlike the products described above, the car ownership rates among Americans in the lowest income decile have remained stubbornly low. Comparing households in the bottom 10 percent and top 10 percent, the inequality gap of access to at least one vehicle remained stubbornly wide from 2014 to 2023.

Households with at least one car

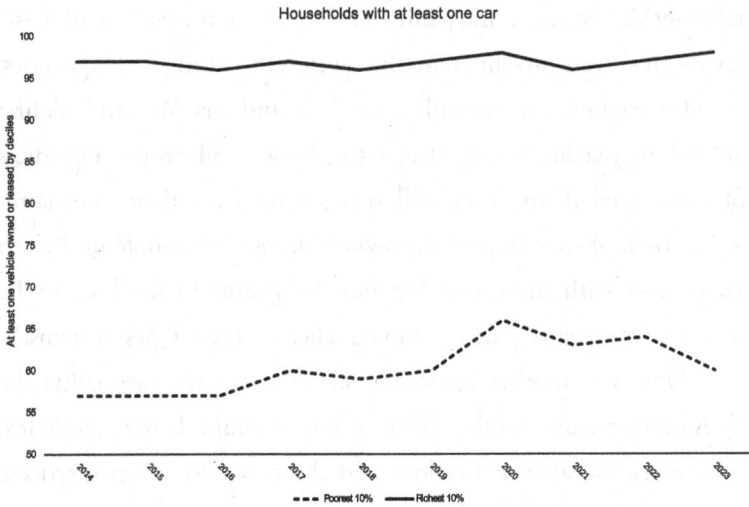

Figure 6-1: Comparison of the poorest 10 percent and the wealthiest 10 percent of Americans who own at least one car, 2014 to 2023.[31]

That is easy to understand when we consider the rising prices of cars and car parts. According to Federal Reserve data, the consumer price index for cars, trucks, and parts—adjusted for inflation—has increased dramatically since 1965. Every added part, every increase in computing power to operate what is essentially an engine and four wheels, contributes to higher costs. Some regulations aimed at making cars more fuel efficient and less polluting forced manufacturers to add complex and expensive equipment. But many other expensive bells and whistles added to cars were driven by the market demand of wealthier consumers. For example, adding sensors to windshields that can assist with braking and steering has increased the cost of replacing a cracked windshield from about $300 to as much as $1500. The higher cost of replacement parts also increases the cost of car insurance. Tariffs in 2025 could also dramatically increase car prices and car parts, furthering inequality in car ownership.

The addition of expensive technology to new cars has caused the prices of *used* cars to remain higher over time. Slower depreciation rates affect low-income households disproportionately. These people often cannot afford a car at all, or they must buy an old car that is more likely to need expensive repairs. As increasing numbers of poorer Americans find themselves priced out of the car market, they sacrifice mobility. Public transportation in American cities is usually pathetic. Many US cities do not even invest in safe bike lanes. Lack of transportation makes it harder for them to find jobs, or it means they must spend longer amounts of time traveling to and from work.

Does Better Efficiency Reduce Inequality?

There is no question that technology can make our use of resources more efficient. The earliest steam engines, which were used to pump water out of British coal mines, operated at about 3 percent efficiency. This means that for every ton of coal burned, about sixty pounds produced the mechanical energy needed to drive the pump. Today, the most efficient combined-cycle coal and gas power plants achieve 40 percent efficiency.

Between the late eighteenth-century and the early nineteenth century, engineers developed ways to improve the efficiency of burning coal, making it more economical. But rather than driving down coal consumption, Britain increased coal usage by a factor of ten. This trend intrigued English economist William Jevons. To him it seemed counterintuitive. Greater efficiency should reduce usage, not increase it, he thought. With further investigation, Jevons found that greater efficiency led to more consumption of coal because the greater efficiency of steam engines drove down the cost of coal. As the Brits burned less coal at the mines, they had more for other uses, such as bigger factories, more trains, and home heating. Increased supply and reduced costs provided economic incentives to produce more coal and to power more machines.

Today, "Jevon's paradox" applies to improvements in automobile fuel efficiency. When a car uses less gasoline, drivers can save money on a per-mile basis, which means they can drive more miles for the same cost. Therefore, improved fuel efficiency might not reduce a nation's overall demand for gasoline. Drivers might use the same amount of fuel simply because they can afford to drive more.

Jevon's paradox also entered public discourse during the 1990s as Intel increased the processing power of their microchips, the company CEO, Andy Grove, postulated that Microsoft (then run by Bill Gates) would produce more complex programs that would gobble up the extra computing power. So, the efficiency gains of computer processors would be used to run more programs rather than to run existing programs faster.

What can Jevon's paradox tell us about modern computing, the rise of artificial intelligence (AI), and economic inequality? First, artificial intelligence is not independently intelligent. Beyond the philosophical and scientific questions about the nature of "intelligence," AI programs must be designed and maintained by humans, and they require human input and oversight. They are entirely dependent on mining, electric grids, and other human-dependent infrastructures. They require troves of human-generated knowledge and information, which the AI companies often steal without regard for copyright laws. Many people work in the industry as low-wage temporary employees with no benefits. It is completely unsurprising that AI companies and their subcontractors would not care about paying fair wages. There is no indication that AI business models are designed to improve reduce income inequality.

Second, AI programs will almost certainly remain in the hands of a small number of large, powerful companies. The true scope and usefulness of AI will be better understood in the coming years, but many small companies and individuals who try to compete with the major players (e.g., OpenAI, Meta, Google, Microsoft) will be forced out of their market niches. As competition dwindles, monopolistic trends will put upward pressure on the cost of AI services. The only possible countervailing trend that might hold this continued stratification in check might be the cost of operating server farms (data centers). These massive installations require large, steady flows of electricity. More critically, server farms require frequent installations of replacement servers. All those servers must be assembled somewhere. The components must be fabricated from materials, including rare earth substances, that must be mined from locations all around the globe. Considering the sprawling supply chains and energy required for AI to work, one starts to wonder if a pen and paper and a human mind might be a better alternative.

If you are like most people, you might experience a sense of dread about the rapid pace of technological change. The frequent disruption makes life feel perpetually uncertain. We sense that a few powerful corporations whose sole aim is economic monopoly impose constant upheaval on us. Daron Acemoglu and Simon Johnson, both MIT economists, describe how major technological changes over the past thousand years have often been sold as "progress," or what they call the "productivity bandwagon," but without regard for the general well-being of individuals.

So, does technology reduce inequality? It depends on how leaders decide to *design* the economic and regulatory frameworks that guide the use of new technologies. In their book *Power and Progress,* Acemoglu and Johnson say there is a direct correlation between the innovators' philosophy and related system of ethics. Humans choose how to design technology, how to use it, and who will benefit from it.

Since at least the 1980s, major technology firms and policymakers have designed economic frameworks that have fueled increased inequality. "Recent research finds that from 1980 onward, automation accelerated; more significantly, there were fewer new tasks and technologies that created opportunities for people," write Acemoglu and Johnson. "This change accounts for much of the deterioration of workers' position in the economy."[32] The authors add that, "Automation and offshoring have raised productivity and multiplied corporate profits, but they have brought nothing resembling shared prosperity to the US," as occurred in the 1950s and 1960s.[33]

Paths for People

If technology will not save us from inequality, and if it tends to *reinforce* inequality in insidious ways, what should ordinary Americans do? Live in a cave and eat tree bark?

There is no denying that the job market is changing rapidly, in part because of the advances and possible advances of artificial intelligence. Many specialists say that AI will revolutionize everything whereas others say that there is a lot of AI hype. Who is right? We do not know. However, college students and young professionals face a lot of uncertainty about which career directions to pursue. Nothing seems certain, but it is important to avoid paralysis and to move forward.

We recommend that young people and mid-career workers learn all they can about artificial intelligence as it pertains to each career interest. For example, search for and read academic journal articles and scholarly books in your field of interest or degree area. Talk to experts, professors, and business leaders in your area to learn more and seek counsel. The goal is to gain as much quality information as possible about how AI company leaders are choosing to impose the technology on society. Look for how these technologies might influence your areas of interest. This information might indicate that you should *not pursue* one path or another. For example, some research shows that AI could do a lot of coding, so it might not be wise to invest time and money to become good at that type of work. Or your search might reveal an opportunity that you had not seen before. Whatever the case, good information is empowering when making big decisions. Knowledge is better than flying blind.

Once you gain sufficient information, you can make a short-term plan, perhaps up to four years. For example, you might choose to pursue a bachelor's degree in a carefully researched area. Make the decision without worrying about a zillion what-ifs. Move forward with your whole heart, complete the degree, have a celebration party, and then reassess. Does the field still look promising? Where are the secure opportunities within each career field in light of changes? Then you can tailor your next steps as needed. Our point is to make a short-term plan, complete that phase, and then build on what you have already done.

It is possible that artificial intelligence will impact labor demand within what we call "digital work" more than jobs in "material" fields. Back in 1983, The Police sang that great song "Spirits in a Material World." They were right. The world is material. People will still need food, clothing, houses, roads, mines, electric transmission cables, and water. We humans will get cavities that need fillings. Most of the world is non-digital. In fact, everything in the digital sphere would not function without physical infrastructure—stuff like copper, salt, sand, and iron.[34] Without copper, there are no electric cables to feed energy to server farms. Amazon would not exist if not for taxpayer-funded roads made of asphalt and concrete. What are the career options within the "material world." Mining engineers? Shipbuilders? Firefighters and nurses?

Third, because we live in a time of rapid change and disruption, we think that it will be increasingly important for families, friends, and community organizations to bond together. We mentioned the importance of relational networks earlier, but the point is worth repeating. People need to rely on each other in times of change. A community provides resilience, enabling individuals to rebound from setbacks and career disruptions. The 1950s rugged individualism will not work out well in our times. A better model is the immigrant families at the beginning of the twentieth century. They benefited by putting three generations under one roof. This allowed them to save money, build capital, and help one another in times of hardship.[35]

Explore your own community to find a mutual aid society or organization to which you can contribute. If this sounds stodgy or old fashioned, all the better. Unlike consumer culture, which is designed to pry every penny from our collective fingers, mutual aid societies can be sources for people within any community to help one another. Try to find an organization that holds regular, in-person meetings, operates within a defined space or community, and offers training of some type. A classic example would be a volunteer fire company. By last count, volunteer fire companies comprise 80 percent of all fire departments in the United States, so one might not be as far away as you think. A volunteer fire company will train new recruits in marketable and tangible skills, including first aid, mechanical troubleshooting, and organizational tactics. They provide opportunities to meet friends and serve the community. And they can be a steppingstone to more advanced positions, such as becoming a paramedic.

Fire companies are just one, quite old, example of a mutual aid society. Others include churches and parent-teacher associations. As the economic system increases inequality, making our revolutionary moment ever more likely, members of mutual-aid societies will offer a safety net. By contrast, atomized people will be less resilient during times of hardship.

How about investing in your mind? We would like to see a

renaissance in the use of classical logic and a deeper understanding of the scientific method. These skills might seem to have a tangential connection to household economics, but we think that critical thinking ability will be crucial in a post-truth age of nefarious propaganda and deep fakes. A solid grounding in the writings of Socrates and Plato will prove invaluable. You can read short pieces like Plato's *Dialogues* that teach foundational skills in basic logic and common fallacies. This type of investment in the mind will help us identify and reject propaganda and marketing intended to convince us to buy products we do not need, or to vote for corrupt and power-hungry political candidates. (Our publisher, Upriver Press, has published a book titled *Overcoming Information Chaos* that provides insights into media literacy in a post-truth age.)

Similarly, we will benefit from a sound understanding of the scientific method: what it does and does not do, and how it aids humanity's investigation of the material world. Too many people think they can "do their own research" about health issues by watching YouTube. Knowing the limits and capabilities of the scientific method as an analytical tool will help everyone spot dubious efforts to push people to drink raw milk, avoid vaccines, or use unproven supplements. The scientific method aids us in building a mental map of a problem, the processes that underlie the process, and, one hopes, a solution.

Finally, we encourage our readers to be engaged citizens. As stated earlier, the economic impact of technology depends on how political leaders and policymakers design frameworks of regulations and laws. So, it pays to team up to push your local, state, and federal politicians to put limits on technologies that threaten the well-being of all Americans.

Paths for Policy

The primary path for policymakers is to dust off the country's antitrust laws. Since the early 1990s, these important laws were rarely, if ever, used to deter the formation of monopolies in the tech sector. At that time, people argued that the courts should not break up the tech companies to ensure that the emerging information technology economy could function in an "interoperable" manner. Everyone needed computing systems and programs to work together so that data could flow smoothly across diverse platforms. Interoperability is like the standardization required for people to drive on highways across states and for trains to travel anywhere in the US; the roads and tracks must be uniform everywhere for the system to work. As the information technology economy developed, everyone wanted to see improvements in what economists call "the network effect," the compatibility needed for one system to interact with another. So, if the government divided up large companies, such as Microsoft, consumers would suffer from the lack of compatibility between a diverse array of computer and software providers. As a result, the courts did not impose antitrust laws.

At that time, this argument made sense. People in the early 1990s were becoming frustrated with the lack of computer compatibility, which caused programs to suddenly crash or prevented data sharing. If programmers said a software program needed exactly 1024 kb of RAM and Windows 95 version 3.12, the programmers meant it. Version 3.02 of Windows 95 running on 512 kb RAM would not function. But thanks to Moore's Law, computing power doubled every twenty-four months. Compatibility improved.

Interoperability barriers gradually fell. These changes allowed the network effect to flourish.

During this period, companies like Microsoft and Apple grew larger and richer, dominating more market share. This raised an obvious question: If we have achieved the network effect and cast aside compatibility barriers, do we still need to allow a few massive companies like Microsoft to retain monopolist control of the software we all depend on for modern communications and data processing? Does it make sense to continue allowing the monopolistic domination of the tech sectors?

In the short term, monopolies seem to offer some benefits. Companies on the road to monopolization can drive down costs for consumers by undercutting competitors. But once the monopolist drives the competition out of business, absolutely nothing short of government action will prevent them from raising prices. Monopoly companies will lumber along while offering products and services with reduced quality, terrible customer service, and no innovation. Worse than that, a monopoly with extremely high market saturation can vertically and horizontally integrate, taking control of entire supply chains and multiple markets.

Vertical integration happens when a company owns all or most links in a supply chain. The company can take a product from raw material inputs to a finished product, and sometimes even to the point of sale, without relying on any third-party providers. An excellent real-world example of vertical integration would be Ford Motor Company's River Rogue complex in Dearborn, Michigan. Completed in 1928, its assembly line stretched a full mile. This facility brought together all facets of producing the Model A and B. Ford shipped raw materials to fabrication shops at one end and finished cars rolled out the other end. All facets of car production were integrated within the company, from one end of the value chain to the other.

Horizontal integration refers to the expansion of a business within the same level of the value chain, typically through a merger or acquisition. This process can happen at the retail level, for example, when one grocery chain buys another. It can also happen earlier in the production process before the final product reaches customers. For instance, a company could buy multiple producers of a good or service within a market, thus expanding market share. They can do this while leaving the public-facing side of the individual brand unchanged. This practice creates an illusion of customer choice when, in fact, one company has expanded its share of the market.

Neither vertical nor horizontal integration are inherently bad. When a company offers a better or cheaper product by controlling the entire supply chain, customers and a company's bottom line can benefit. As for horizontal integration, the acquisition of one company by another company may not upset the competitive balance in a market—*if* the new company does not control too much market share. At some point, the practice turns from healthy competition to market domination.

The real problems come about when a single company achieves both features; that is, when horizontal and vertical integration gives a company total control of the production process and all the steps in the value chain. Wal-Mart is a perfect example of this. With their house brands, in-house logistics, and monopolistic pricing power, Wal-Mart managed to destroy most locally owned retail grocers in America. In the fourth quarter of 2023, the company controlled almost 43.8 percent of the US retail market. Their nearest rival,

Costco, controls about 17.8 percent of the retail market, followed by Home Depot at about 10.9 percent, then Target at 7.7 percent, and then Lowes with 6.2 percent of the retail market.

While these companies fight for retail dominance in the brick-and-mortar world, they have all decisively lost the struggle to control the e-commerce market. In 2023, Wal-Mart tallied $1.1 billion in online sales. That number is paltry in comparison to Amazon's online sales numbers. Amazon accounts for 37.6 percent of all online sales in the United States. Roughly two of every five dollars spent online happens on the Amazon website. This situation has made Amazon stockholders rich, but no one else.

The lackluster application of antitrust laws amounts to yet another form of inequality by design. We would ask citizens and policymakers alike to ask one essential question: Is this outsized control of the retail market good for customers, workers, or the country? At what point should we, as a nation, draw the line?

As this book goes to press in early 2025, two major antitrust efforts indicate that the government intends to curtail thirty years of monopoly trends in the technology sector. A case against Google that began in September 2024 under the Biden Administration ended in mid-April 2025. The court ruled against Google, stating "that Google violated antitrust law by monopolizing open-web digital advertising markets. According to the court, Google 'harmed Google's publishing customers, the competitive process, and, ultimately, consumers of information on the open web.'"[36]

The second antitrust case was brought by the Federal Trade Commission against Meta, owned by billionaire Mark Zuckerberg, after a six-year investigation into whether the social media giant could legally own Instagram and WhatsApp. One news report summed the case up this way: "At stake is the future of Meta's $1.4 trillion advertising business and the prospect of having to spin off its hugely popular services into separate companies—a corporate breakup the likes of which has not been seen since AT&T's telephone monopoly was forced to split apart more than forty years ago."[37]

These cases could be helpful, but with the rise of artificial intelligence, a small number of massive tech companies could end up controlling all information flow in the US, if not in the world. Policymakers must put guardrails on these platforms now to prevent the monopolization of the entire information landscape.

CHAPTER 7

The Cooperative Ownership Solution

Many pundits spill a lot of digital ink dismissing the reality of America's economic inequality. In that context, people share all kinds of opinions about pay ratios. Does the CEO make too much? Is the janitor not paid enough? How much should minimum wage be? What is a "fair" wage? How much wealth does the 1 percent have compared to the 99 percent? Should we even have billionaires? Should we institute a wealth tax on every cent made after $999,999,999 and redistribute it directly to taxpayers?

These questions require us to consider factors such as inflation, purchasing power, and worker productivity before we can calculate what we mean by "fair wage." The dizzying array of variables affecting inputs and outcomes becomes such a mess that one might yearn for an Alexander the Great to come along, swing a sword, and cut the Gordian Knot. In other words, people might want a dictator. (Always a horrible idea.) Is there a way to bypass the punditry and chaos, and implement a system that is fair for average workers?

Marxists would say, yes, there is a way to build a fair system and it involves red banners. We tried that experiment during the twentieth century and the result was millions of deaths, famines, war, and mass poverty. In economic terms, the record is clear: state ownership of business produces lethargic economies that do not foster the entrepreneurial spirit or keep food on tables and clothing on backs. So, is that the end of the discussion? Capitalism won and communism failed, right?

Yes, communism failed, but that failure does not mean that capitalism is flawless. Global capitalism functions as the default model for running the world economy, but does that mean there are no other ways to organize an economy? In this chapter, we look carefully at the model of business cooperatives, which could be a means for reducing inequality while promoting a healthier form of capitalism.

A Spanish Success

Let us take a quick trip to the Basque region of northern Spain. There, a firm started by six men in 1956 has expanded and evolved into the Mondragón Cooperative Corporation (MCC). Partly in reaction to the suppression of their language and culture under the Franco dictatorship, partly inspired by the priest Don Jose Maria, and partly to imagine a free market system that was not so ruthlessly exploitative, these six men grew their business from a single shop into a network of co-ops. In 2022, the MCC generated revenue of €12 billion, employed about seventy-five thousand people, and operated 260 companies and cooperatives. The MCC rates as the sixth largest manufacturing organization in Spain.

What does this have to do with the tired debate between the proponents of unbridled, rapacious corporate oligarchy and the apologists for Marxism and mass-murdering police states? In the paragraph above, we used the word *cooperative* for good reason. The employees of the MCC own the firm. Technically, they own whatever local cooperative they work for. The 260 or so cooperatives function together as a conglomerate. In addition, the MCC operates a credit union (called La Caja) that provides capital for new MCC enterprises and oversees the retirement pensions for all seventy-six thousand employees. The credit union also serves as the financial channel for distributing profits to the workers. Approximately 70 percent of net profits flows to the employees each year, with 20 percent held as capital (reserved by the credit union), and 10 percent put into an employee pension plan.

Mondragón does not limit themselves to manufacturing and finance. In accordance with Don Jose's vision, education is a cornerstone of the cooperative corporation. The MCC also operates a Polytechnic University that keeps the workers educated, equipping them to adapt to changing times. When new technologies or management techniques emerge, the Polytechnic University diffuses these ideas throughout the cooperative corporation. Book learning and profit sharing is great, but how do the shops operate on a day-to-day basis?

The Mondragón model involves workplace democracy. This does not mean that every shop decision gets put to a vote, and it does not involve weekly meetings. Instead, the MCC shop managers are usually elected from the ranks of the workers, and they serve on an annual basis. Occasionally, the MCC will hire managers from outside the cooperative network, but this generally happens when a shop fails for several years to generate a profit or maintain productivity. Managers pursue a cooperative relationship with employees, but they can be recalled or voted out every year.

For bigger picture issues, like industry trends and strategic redirection of the cooperative corporation, the workers elect representatives to an annual general assembly. The assembly sets broader MCC policy, addresses any needed leadership changes, and functions to keep information about the bigger picture flowing to the specific shops.

In summary, the MCC proves that worker cooperatives can become multibillion dollar companies. Could this serve as a model for running a local diner or corner store? What can this example teach America?

Objections to Worker Cooperatives

The cooperative model is not new, but for most Americans it is unfamiliar, so it *seems* new. When we encounter new ideas, we often think about their potential problems or pitfalls. That is good. Critical thinking is better than gullibility. Any good idea is often made better by legitimate good-faith criticism. However, in relation to new ideas for economic and business models, many people have become skeptical of everything. That sentiment is understandable, but our current crony capitalist system is extremely detrimental to the well-being of Americans. So, we need to try something new, something akin to the Mondragón cooperative model.

To be fair, we should first present and respond to the criticisms of the MCC approach. One reasonable argument against worker co-ops comes from the finance sector. In the real-world experience of organizations like Mondragón, traditional sources of capital—banks, pension funds, and other financial investment firms—shy away from entities that retain the profits in-house. From one perspective, this makes sense. If workers retain the profits and reinvest them in the firm or in the credit unions that back the firms, there would not be much money left for investors. Thus, it is not hard to imagine a worker co-op failing to attract traditional lenders. Add to this the philosophical underpinning of the worker cooperative, which is that labor should create wealth for the workers and their communities rather than shareholders. So, it is easy to see why traditional sources of finance would shy away from investing in worker co-ops.

Mondragón deals with this problem by setting up credit unions into which the company deposits a percentage of profits. This requires workers to maintain a level of savings. By doing so, Mondragón has been able to provide capital for expansion, retooling, and reinvestment. In the late 1970s and 1980s Mondragón's cooperatives frequently received government support from Basque provincial authorities, which aided investment and capitalization. So, the MCC story shows that financing a worker cooperative is doable outside of the world of traditional finance, but it is also not a story of laissez-faire capitalism.

The cooperative framework has no barriers against floating traditional corporate bonds or taking on traditional debt from banking houses. Mondragón co-ops have pursued traditional finance from time to time. According to scholarly research, the returns that the MCC offered to traditional bankers were rarely enough to entice traditional investment. That said, it is fair to say that obtaining traditional forms of investment could be the biggest hurdle faced by Americans who wish to start a co-op or employee-owned company.

Critics also rightly point out that worker cooperatives operate less nimbly than owner-dominated businesses, which are the business models that most Americans would be familiar with in the private sector. In these companies, the shareholders or managers make all the decisions. All the choices about hiring and firing, setting wages, deciding compensation packages and day-to-day operations flow from the top-down. The obvious upside of such a business model is that it allows a well-informed manager or owner to make quick decisions and implement them unilaterally. Any organization with one decision-maker can move much more quickly than a business that requires cooperation or consent. In the context of a financial crisis, the organization that acts quickly may be the organization that survives.

The drawbacks of managerial unilateralism become obvious when one considers the broader context of modern America. Over the past thirty years, it has become an axiom in Silicon Valley that any good business moves fast and breaks stuff. Originally, people believed that companies must innovate or die. Silicon Valley leaders referred to the concept with the phrase "creative destruction" (they did not coin the term). Functionally, however, many Silicon Valley companies (and others) sought to destroy other businesses in the hopes that whatever new model came out of the ashes would be inherently better.

Given the wreckage that Silicon Valley has made of many economies, both local and national, we do not think the creative destruction model is useful for running an economy, in part because it drives monopolization. The business cooperative model might be more conservative and slower to adapt, but it conserves a productive economy and the well-being of workers. Those outcomes could be better than rapid change in the name of efficiency. The creative destruction model puts American workers in shark-infested waters without a life vest.

Has the creative destruction model improved society? Consider the effects of this business model on taxi services. According to a 2022 survey, one of every seven gig drivers who works for companies like Gruhub, Uber, Lyft, and DoorDash make less than the Federal minimum wage of $7.50 per hour. One in four works for less than the minimum wage of the state in which each driver lives. About 30 percent of those drivers qualify for SNAP benefits, formerly known as food stamps. Unsurprisingly, two-thirds of gig drivers make less than $15 per hour. This may be OK for someone who wants to earn extra money on the side for a few hours a week, but for those trying to earn a full-time living, this supposedly flexible form of employment only reinforces economic inequality. Workers are sold the idea that they can set their own hours and be their own bosses, but they are still required to work long hours for low pay and no benefits. Who gets rich? The "creative" destructors.

Worker cooperatives, on the other hand, have incentives to move slowly, to *not break things,* and to maintain what is good for employees and society. Worker cooperatives are slower to respond to market forces and conditions, but they are deliberate about long-term outcomes. As described earlier, the MCC emphasizes manager training and adaptation to market trends while simultaneously retraining workers whose jobs have been made redundant by technology. This is not a business model that seeks to emulate the social or economic structures of the 1950s. Rather, worker cooperatives have an incentive to support workers and remain invested in their communities. This model does not exist in twenty-first century oligarchic America.

Another critique of worker cooperatives is that they might be hesitant to invest in innovative technology if doing so would result in layoffs. Here again we can look at how the world's largest worker cooperative handles decisions about advanced technologies. Mondragón invests in them, but it does this while also investing in worker retraining. The MCC is better at retraining workers than profit-maximizing US corporations or government workforce retraining programs. Traditional American businesses, driven by the creative disruption ownership class, just tell workers whose jobs have been eliminated by technology to learn to code. Now AI might eliminate the need for coders. So, that line will not work much longer. In the 1990s, the MCC retrained and moved workers from cooperatives that were losing 50 percent of their workforce to cooperatives that needed new workers. This stands in stark contrast to the laissez-faire model adopted in the United States where businesses simply fire workers and tell them to look for a government retraining program, if one exists where they live.

In addition to these objections, worker cooperatives face barriers in relation to the broader banking and Federal Reserve system. Credit availability is largely controlled by the Federal Reserve as it seeks to manage interest rates, money supply, and employment levels. Two factors, at least, can make it difficult for cooperatives to obtain credit at reasonable rates. First, the people who chair the twelve regional Federal Reserve boards and oversee the Fed's implementation policy come directly from the leadership of large banks. Second, the Fed operates under a legal mandate to control inflation, so its leadership consistently skews inflation targeting policies in favor large lenders and borrowers.

The Federal Reserve system is not a public institution run by the United States Government. Rather, it operates as a quasi-public bank that is owned by banks that participate in its framework. The regional boards of the Federal Reserve are composed of banking and commercial interests that select the president and executives of each regional Fed and ultimately the members of the Federal Open Market Committee (FOMC). The US president and Congress may choose the Fed chair and seven governors, but the banks who own and participate in the Federal Reserve system select the regional presidents. Smaller institutions and credit unions may be shut out based on the rules of the game that have been established by the large banks.

Small banks that enter the regulatory framework of the Federal Reserve agree to be overseen by an institution that is owned by their largest competitors. One might ask why smaller banks would participate in this system. The answer to that question, for most small banks, would be to receive regulatory support and Fed stimulus should a nationwide economic crisis break out. Small and midsize banks need a credible and supportive partner to face the ebb and flow of the business cycle. The most well-known support system is the Federal Deposit Insurance Commission (FDIC). If your local bank fails but participates in the FDIC, then you, as a depositor, will have full access to the funds in your accounts.

The Fed has shown that, as an institution, its actions are unfavorable to small banks, even in the case of a "rescue stimulus." The behind-the-scenes way the FDIC works involves moving the assets of a failing bank, chiefly its deposits and non-toxic loans, from the books of the failing bank to a larger institution. Theoretically, the receiving institution could be any size, but the historical record shows that the wealth held by small banks usually transfers to the big banks. So, to ask the question again, why would any small bank participate in a system designed for its demise? Because small banks have no other choice. Just as small retailers must increasingly deal with Amazon to their own detriment, small banks and credit unions have been at a disadvantage to the big players who own the majority stake in our Federal Reserve system.

The carrot for small banks to participate in the system is FDIC insurance. But there is also a stick. Consider the Four Corners Credit Union in Colorado. This specialty lender provides banking services for marijuana dispensaries, which is legal in Colorado but not at the federal level. In this case, the Kansas City Regional Fed rejected the bank's application for legal reasons; however, the Fed has the power to reject *any* bank or credit union for *any* reason. If the Bank of America leadership, for example, wanted to deny a credit union operated by cooperatives, they could find a way to push it out of the system either by denial of service or by influencing regulatory agents. Perhaps a regional Fed board would argue that a business, like a cooperative, could not operate a credit union under the same roof.

Another factor that drives inequality in the banking sector is the expansionary policy of the Fed. Mark Cuban cheekily called this policy "universal basic income for rich people." Perhaps it is better to call it universal basic income for rich banks. As the Fed expands the money supply, it first buys assets from "primary dealers" that comprise a list of twelve to fifteen large national and international banks like Santander, Deutsche Bank, and Goldman Sachs. These primary dealers are then expected to lend money to small banks, such as Commerce Bank or the Bank of Oklahoma. However, because there is no legal requirement to support small banks, the large banks often take a pass. During the Great Recession, the asset balance sheets of large banks exploded while smaller banks suffered and died.

The Fed has been instrumental in supporting the continued "increasing returns to scale" of the financial system. In other words, the Fed has propped up the increasingly monopolistic behavior of large banks. Hopefully, this outcome is an *unintentional* consequence of their monetary policy. Taken to its extreme, the largest five banks will continue to outcompete and buy out smaller banks until they are the only ones standing. According to Federal Reserve data, there were more than fourteen thousand commercial banks in the US in 1980. As of 2020, there were only four thousand commercial banks. These remaining banks are competing in a "Financial Thunder Dome," but in the coming years, it is possible that only four or five monster banks will remain.

Why Cooperatives Can Be Profitable

Now that we have discussed some of the points that might speak against worker cooperatives, it is worth talking about their benefits. First, remember that in a typical American business model, the owners receive most of the profits. The employees work long hours and receive almost none of the profit.

A cooperative can organize the division of labor however it wants, but these cooperatives typically do not pay all employees the same rate. For example, the MCC pays those in senior management or in positions of greater responsibility more than those with lesser or more narrowly defined roles. However, the MCC shares the profits among the people who produce the profits: the workers. Unlike corporations in the US, they do not ship the profits to corporate headquarters for the benefit of executives and shareholders who will never see the shop floors or meet the people who generated their wealth. As stated earlier, Mondragón directly reinvests 10 percent of profits to the pension fund operated by La Caja (the MCC's credit union), then 20 percent of the profits go toward recapitalizing accounts, which allows the business to invest in new equipment during the next fiscal year. The lion's share, 70 percent of the profits, flows directly to the employees of the business or co-op.

For the sake of comparison, imagine what might have happened if, in fiscal year 2022, Apple shared its profits with its employees. Publicly reported numbers show that Apple employed 164,000 people that year.[38] The company made net profits of $88.5 billion.[39] This means that each employee, as an average, created about $539,634 in one year. If we use the MCC's 1 to 2:7 ratio for profit sharing, Apple employees would have received $377,744 in 2022.

We acknowledge that most businesses are not as profitable as Apple, but it is not the only company making gigantic profits on a per-employee basis. For example, in 2020 Visa reported a profit of $10.9 billion. The company employed 20,500 workers, so the per-worker profit was $530,049. Meta Platforms that same year reported profits of $29.1 billion and employed 58,604 workers. This means that the per-worker profit was $497,338.[40] Do you think workers received a fair share of those profits?

Beyond Authoritarian Control

Of course, more than just money makes the world go round. Power relationships, including among businesses, form a bedrock of human societies. All human endeavors rely on group cohesion to achieve a result greater than the sum of the parts. Within hierarchies, which are the most common form of organizational structure in corporate America (and in the military), upper-level people must rely on lower-level people to do the work. Workplaces combine hierarchies with the division of labor to produce goods and services that no one person could manage alone.

Despite the myth of the "exceptional individual" who can do everything alone, human beings always achieve more in groups. The examples are boundless. Doctors rely on nurses, techs, and secretaries to deliver patient care. No singer, no matter how talented the voice, can tour without a backup band, road crew, producers, and marketers. Regardless of the industry, people achieve greater economic activity, and produce more goods and services for their societies when they work together.

Now that we live in industrial societies with global supply chains that link harvest with table and raw materials with finished good, it seems more important than ever to acknowledge the reality of hierarchies and the importance of individuals who work in the broader system. The problem with today's industrial model is that it usually functions by coercion. Unlike workers in previous generations, today's labor force must survive with scant employee protections. A hyper-capitalist system pushes down wages and sends profits to the C-suite. When our bosses tell us to jump, we do not even ask "how high?" We just jump.

The perception of powerlessness created by such a coercive system can be seen across American society. According to a March 2025 survey conducted by Pew Research, nearly 40 percent of all American workers are unsatisfied with their jobs. Low pay in relation to the cost of living is the most prominent reason for this dissatisfaction. About 80 percent of all workers say their pay is not keeping up with the cost of living. Less than half of all employees say they are happy with company-provided benefits, and close to 80 percent say they have no opportunities for promotion.[41] Some of these perspectives probably reflect standard bellyaching, but it is also true that people are working for less compared to previous generations, as we discussed earlier in the book. Employers are placing more weight on workers' shoulders with absolutely none of the broader social rewards that a stable job might have conferred on a person in generations past. This is what the hierarchical system offers workers.

Workers' cooperatives offer a better alternative, but they still retain hierarchical elements of business governance. The MCC in Spain is not a hyper-democratic workplace in which everyone shows up in the morning and votes on what job they want to do. Employees are expected to complete the tasks given to them by the managers. However, Mondragón distributes more power to workers while simultaneously empowering the managers. This is accomplished through a mechanism called a general assembly. Members of individual cooperatives select delegates who meet once a year at the general assembly. The goal is to chart a course for the larger corporation over the coming year and to make decisions about promoting, hiring, demoting, and, if need be, firing managers. This system serves to reinforce the cooperative nature of the model, as opposed to using coercion.

Again, Mondragón's shops are not chaotic small workplaces where anything goes, where there are no rules, and where nothing gets done. In the run up to Spain's admission to the European Economic Community in the early 1990s, Mondragón's general assembly recognized that their cooperatives would need to step up their game if they wanted to compete with the giant top-down corporations that dominated the European economy. However, the MCC did not choose to adopt a top-down coercive model; instead, they stuck with the cooperative model, knowing that it produced better tangible results for workers *and* the bottom line.

In the US, workers' cooperatives will need to be understood within the broader context of labor relations. People often confuse this model with unionization, but cooperatives are distinct. The history of US labor relations begins with the founding of the fledgling Republic during the Enlightenment era. The Founders enshrined property rights and individual rights in the Bill of Rights and the US Constitution. By the time industrialization really got going in the 1840s, property rights were prominently enshrined in the legal system. This produced mixed results. For instance, in the states north of the Mason-Dixon line, property rights created a substantial class of yeoman who ran small farms, and a class of merchants who ran cottage industries. South of the Mason-Dixon line, property rights created a class of big landowners who jealously guarded the right to exploit chattel slaves and to treat those people as private property. These regional differences led to disputes over what constituted "property," and how far the Federal government could go in the regulation of property rights. This dispute culminated in the Civil War after the 1860 election. Mixed results, indeed.

After the war, industrialization spread rapidly across the North and even made inroads into the formerly agrarian-dominated South. As industrialization picked up steam, most cottage industries in the northern states went out of business. Former cottage industry workers from the North moved to search for work, which set the stage for decades of labor unrest. Those who controlled the capital used the legal system and a very compliant political class to enforce the primacy of private property rights at the expense of personal rights. State governments derailed any attempt by workers to demand higher wages, shorter work weeks, or safer working conditions. Unions during the Progressive Era of the early 1910s and again during the Great Depression in the 1930s helped, but the relationship between workers and management was always adversarial. During the past five decades, US policymakers and CEOs have mostly worked to de-unionize the nation. Toward the end of the Biden administration, there were some unionization efforts, such as within Starbucks and Amazon.

It is generally true that unionized workers enjoy higher wages, better benefits, and less onerous work schedules. The importance of unions should not be dismissed or sidelined, but their accomplishments are a story of conflict with business owners. Workers and employers all assume that they must oppose each other.

This is where the cooperative model has potential to shine. In such a system, workers exercise real power in their workplaces. They share in the profits, but they also shoulder the dangers if the business cannot turn a profit. Everyone is in the same boat. Because individuals thrive best in close-knit groups, cooperatives offer the greatest chance of success. As a network, they can call on each other for help in the down years, and they can support each other in the good years. Everyone becomes more resilient, including businesses. Workers experience better financial returns, improved relationships with their superiors, and less stress.

If the US widely adopted such a system, it would also greatly reduce inequality while remaining clearly within a capitalist framework. Wealth and control would shift away from the concentrated centers of banking and boardrooms and toward those who produce all the wealth with their sweat and tears. It might take a decade or more, but converting major employers from capital-ownership to worker-ownership structures might be the single largest reform that could reverse economic inequality.

Paths for People

We encourage our readers to push companies, business leaders, policymakers, and elected officials to study and implement the cooperatives model described above. It has been overlooked for too long in the US. Cooperatives do not have to be formed solely for the purpose of business enterprises. For instance, rural electric co-ops already form the backbone of electricity service in many rural areas of the US. These ventures were not set up as profit-seeking businesses; instead, they allow rural populations to buy electricity at a wholesale rate and then, once maintenance and operations costs are covered, resell that electricity at less-than-retail prices.

Cooperatives can also be formed to serve any economic need, if there are enough parties willing to shoulder the costs and reap the benefits. As the wider American economy becomes increasingly dominated by a handful of firms in any given sector, co-ops could and should be able to fend off monopoly power by linking cottage-scale producers with customers.

In the meantime, perhaps the most obvious way that Americans can improve the outlook for workers is to push for unionization. Historically, unions provide the best way for an individual to secure something that approximates fair pay and benefits in exchange for labor. People who apply at nonunion shops must negotiate pay and benefits. This may work out okay for people with skill sets that are in high demand in a context of low supply, but most people end up accepting lower wages just to ensure they have work, especially during recessions.

To combat this downward pressure on wages, workers can engage in "market differentiation" to regain some pricing power. They can convince the employer to pay more by showing, for example, that they have an advanced degree, a certification or license in a trade, or many years of experience. But this kind of signaling and market differentiation can be costly for workers who must spend more time and money earning, for example, higher degrees.

Another solution is for governments to set a credible and enforceable fixed price (minimum wage) that restores what would have been the efficient competitive wage. Alternatively, workers can get together and negotiate as a collective for higher wages. In effect the suppliers of labor can negotiate for higher wages by creating their own enforceable agreement without the government. The advantage of this latter solution is that workers take ownership of their labor rather than relying on government.

Instability in the labor market is an often-overlooked negative outcome of our current approach to labor relations. Talk to business owners and employees, and they will usually say that there is very little loyalty between them. Companies will quickly downsize their staffs in temporary recessions. Likewise, employees will quickly jump ship if they find a job that pays a little more. This creates instability for workers and employers. As a result, the employers end up investing in hiring and training new employees who soon leave for rival firms. This so-called "churn" is built into the American business model and into the mindset of at least three generations. We should not be surprised to hear younger generations report that they have tenuous loyalty to their employers. Why should they when loyalty is based on coercion and/or returned with exploitation?

Unionization also protects workers against arbitrary firing and punitive discipline. As a former union steward, one of this book's authors can attest to the importance of having someone in the room to make sure employees are disciplined or fired according to the contract, not according to the whims of an aggrieved middle manager. That is not to say that every employee is blameless; some people should be fired, but when employers know they have the upper hand in all labor-management relations, they have little incentive to abide by labor contracts or engage in fair hearings.

Paths for Policy

Much to our chagrin, the paths for individuals are always riddled with roadblocks set up by those who benefit from the existing economic order. These barriers might take the form of tax codes designed to benefit those who can afford a high-priced CPA and lawyer, or they might be the outright subsidies that flow to the largest firms, or they might be state and local ordinances that are impossible for small companies to comply with. In early 2025, as the Trump administration rolled out sweeping tariffs, many small businesses and farmers wondered if they would be able to survive. As a result, we need a conversation about policy-level changes.

Remember that all laws are just agreed-upon principles. Some laws, like the prohibition against murder and the state monopoly over violence, have deep roots in common law and religious tradition. Others are products of their time. The legal principle that a corporation can outlast the legal mandate that set it up goes back to the 1880s. Before then, corporations were established for a specific economic goal, such as building a canal and transferring the profits from that venture to the investors. These types of limits on corporations existed until the 1886 Supreme Court case *Santa Clara County v. Southern Pacific Railroad*. The court found that fourteenth amendment protections applied to corporations. Since then, courts have repeatedly reaffirmed this protection. However, it is incorrect to say that fourteenth amendment protections for corporations are rooted in a long history of customs and religious observance.

Imagine a scenario in which US elected officials decided to chart a different course, one that balanced the needs of people with the desire of the few to profit. (Take a moment to laugh.) There are ways that a legislature could rebalance the economic scales. These legal proposals would not require the US Congress to act. State lawmakers could pass laws with the following proposals in mind.

Overturn "Corporate Personhood" Laws

We recommend a law that transfers the ownership of firms above a certain size to the employees. Such a law would shift profits to the employees (the new owners of the firms), but the law would also place more risk on the employees by making them responsible for business governance. Such a reform would grant average workers more agency over their economic futures, and it would discredit the idea that high-level owners and managers in corner offices have superior intellect, work ethic, or moral purity. Americans often believe a shibboleth that those who rise to the top of the economic food chain are better than everyone who does not. In a curious way, the boardrooms of corporate America have adopted the passive/active citizen distinction that was embedded in the French Constitution of 1789. French leaders at that time believed that only men who owned property and who were at least age twenty-five could vote or serve in the legislative assembly. Does this attitude sound familiar in the twenty-first century economy?

Lawmakers, even at the state level, could give ownership and voting control back to workers by overturning or at least limiting "corporate personhood" laws. Passing these laws would require a carrot and a stick. For the current wealthy owners of large corporations, the carrot would be to *not revisit* the forty years of excesses and wealth accumulation. Let bygones be bygones. The stick would be a legal principle called *revocationism*. If the people in charge of a corporation, limited liability company, or any other legal entity refused to transfer ownership of the business to worker control, the legal rights of that business would face revocation. No longer could company boards or shareholders hide behind "corporate personhood" protections that exempt them from personal responsibility for business actions. If a power company refuses to transfer ownership to workers, and if the existing owners allow millions of pounds of fly ash to pollute a watershed, then the existing owners would be liable for the downstream damage. If a railroad chooses not to invest in up-to-date safety equipment, and if that decision resulted in a derailment that contaminated an entire community, the shareholders would be personally liable for covering the health care costs of harmed individuals for the next twenty years. If Immigration and Customs Enforcement (ICE) busts a facility for employing undocumented immigrants, the business owners who were responsible for hiring decisions would be subject to criminal prosecution as an accessory to breaking immigration law.

This legal stick would certainly encourage current business owners to transfer ownership to workers. Lawmakers would need to study how to handle franchise chains under such a law, if for no other reason than to close a potential loophole that large retailers might try to exploit. We can imagine Wal-Mart trying to make each store operate as an independent "small business."

We do not think that small businesses should be subject to this proposal. Most official measures classify a small business as having no more than five hundred employees. We think that the number should be no more than fifty employees; however, if we use the official number, then small businesses employ 46 percent of the private-sector workforce in the US. They do not cause income inequality, in part because they do not hoard substantial amounts of wealth.

Stronger Regulation of the Financial Sector

Perhaps no other sector of the economy is a greater engine of inequality than the financial sector; nevertheless, it is subject to minimal regulations and public oversight. In our view, US lawmakers should start by reinstating the Great Depression-era law called the Glass-Stegall Act, which legally separated commercial banking from investment banking. Without this law, the financial sector has had the freedom to concentrate wealth in the upper income brackets. The financialization of the US economy means that the end users of credit (average borrowers and small businesses) pay all the costs. Meanwhile, those with access to the Federal Reserve's banking window reap all the profits.

Our proposed reforms would level the playing field for workers and small businesses by focusing on big businesses, banks, and the financial sector. There is nothing "communist" about our ideas. Improving government regulations is not the same as the state taking over companies. Private companies could still operate as before; they would simply lack the legal and financial safety nets that give them the upper hand on the economic playing field. These reforms would take time to implement, and the effects may take a generation, but by pushing profits and economic control back down the ladder to the American people, we could steer the ship of state away from the iceberg of political violence.

CHAPTER 8

If It Is Broke, Fix It

"No one cares, so work harder." That phrase has surged in popularity in recent years. Those who spread it around social media want to emphasize the value of hard work, but those words could also have been spoken by feudal lords or slave owners. No employers today see themselves as feudal lords or slave drivers, but such chatter makes people think that America's political economy should operate solely as a meritocracy.

Underneath this phrase are dark assumptions: a human life has an easily defined value; the value of a person derives solely from productive output; and the broader society is not responsible for those who have fallen into tough times. The assumption is that sickness, leisure, grief, and tragedy are personal problems that no one else should care about. The important thing is to work more. A person with the flu should show up to work. A person should give up every weekend for overtime. A person cannot mourn a loss if it interferes with work. Work must come before all other things. Such sentiments corrode a person's soul.

People in ancient hunter-gatherer tribes assumed that everyone should contribute to the survival of the tribe. From this vantage point, one wonders if the "no one cares, so work harder" mantra might be the most *unnatural and idiotic* idea for a social contract ever conceived. But that phrase encapsulates the attitude of the 1 percent toward the rest of us. In their view, we are simply cogs in a machine. So, work until you break. And when you do break, no one will care.

In this chapter, we move away from a numbers-driven analysis to a qualitative analysis, which is equally important because it focuses on the narratives that influence Americans' collective imagination and cultural worldview. Economists sometimes shy away from such topics because they do not involve the perceived objectivity of numbers. But countries and economies are driven by people who make personal decisions based on what they believe and the values they hold dear. These beliefs and values are shaped by personal history, upbringing, and other factors such as media and education. If people assume society is rigid, exploitative, unjust, or cruel, they will make economic decisions that are in line with their beliefs about the broader society.

Here is a fact: The political economy of the United States has reached a breaking point. We stand at a crossroads in the history of our culture. Many citizens are asking whether the constitutional American project is worth it. They increasingly doubt whether hard work will even be enough to keep a roof over their heads or keep their families alive. In many cases, the answer to those questions looks increasingly like a definitive no.

In the previous chapters we showed that inequality is at the root of many Americans' despair and malaise. This did not occur overnight. Like the concrete still curing at the center of the Hoover Dam, economic inequality grows stronger every day. Like the Hoover Dam, which was a public works project that provided jobs during the Great Depression, inequality is a "dam" that reduces the flow of widespread economic gains, channeling wealth to a small group. Anyone who tours the Hoover Dam will learn from the guide that one day the dam will start to falter. The dam of inequality—

which was built by design—will also begin to break down. When the cracks appear, the dam can go from stability to complete failure quite quickly. All of us will have to contend with the chaos left by the deluge. Those living directly below the dam will not have to contend with it for long.

Why Do Nations Fail?

In their groundbreaking book titled *Why Nations Fail*, economists Darren Acemoglu and James Robinson examined why some nations are poor, why some are rich, and what factors allow a nation to move from one category to the other. A dominant factor of economic success or failure, they write, is the presence of strong institutions that guarantee the rule of law and the broader social contract. The first prerequisite seems obvious. After all, why would a company invest in an economic project that could end up falling apart because there are no governing institutions to provide stability and fair rules. The second point, which is about sustaining the social contract, is more abstract but no less important. Why would an individual invest in education or entrepreneurship when the rules of society offer little assurance that the time and effort will be backed by systems that recognize the value of education, work, and property rights? Acemoglu and Robinson examined this relationship in reverse to ascertain whether rich countries simply *bought* good institutions or whether the institutions themselves made the nations rich. They found that a robust legal system and strong, inclusive institutions are prerequisites to economic growth. Without a good government, a prosperous economy will not emerge or survive.

Acemoglu and Robinson present a spectrum on which all political economic systems fall. This spectrum ranges from highly inclusive to highly extractive. A society with institutions that protect the property rights of broad sections of society beyond just the elites can be classified as *inclusive*. This type of economy will foster broad-based economic growth. Inclusive institutions allow individuals to participate in the wider economy and profit from that inclusion. On the other hand, extractive political-economic systems exclude large segments of the population from property rights, and they funnel profits to elites at the expense of all others in a society.

These two scholars found a causal link between colonialism and extractive economic systems, which is not a surprise. Despite Victorian-era propaganda, the British set up the Raj to run India and, frankly, to steal everything that was not nailed down. They did this rather than provide the good people of the Indian subcontinent with well-run institutions and a civilization. Many empires set up colonies to pump wealth back to the imperial center (e.g., Spain, Portugal, France), but when the colonies achieved independence, the new leaders found themselves in charge of post-colonial economies that had been designed for exploitation rather than for fostering healthy businesses. By contrast, colonial states that required a large diaspora of people to do the demanding work of building the place tended to produce independent countries that went on to become rich. The authors compare the outcomes in North and South Korea to illustrate the importance of democratic (inclusive) institutions. They also hold up the historical example of the Glorious Revolution in Great Britain to emphasize the importance of inclusive institutions.

Today, the United States is at risk of sliding away from a

democracy based on rule-of-law and good governance. Over the last forty years, policymakers in corporate boardrooms and the halls of Congress gradually have undermined the foundations of our success. By removing laws and regulations against the unlimited expansion of large businesses, laissez-faire and neoliberal policies have fostered an explosion of monopolistic firms and markets controlled by a handful of players. These powerful individuals and corporations set prices for primary producers and end consumers. To take just one example, consider the meatpacking sector for beef. Just four companies control an estimated 85 percent of the US beef packing market.[42] The same consolidation has occurred among banks, airlines, and insurance companies. Unregulated markets lead to the "natural" formation of monopolistic firms with dominant market power. Ironically, the idealized economic policy of allowing the free market to pick winners and losers resulted not in greater competition, but in the monopolization of entire economic sectors, which ends the free market that was supposed to foster competition.

In many nations, and increasingly in the US, the rule of law is applied heavily against average citizens who step out of line. By contrast, people who have enough money to hire expensive lawyers or to bankroll the political campaigns of well-placed judges and senators can break the law with impunity or by paying a small fine, which is seen as the cost of doing business. Wells Fargo, the third largest bank in the United States, was alleged to have opened fraudulent accounts for more than sixteen million customers and then illegally charged erroneous fees and interest charges on auto and home loans, as well as unlawful overdraft fees.[43] The Consumer Financial Protection Bureau, a watchdog agency set up in the wake of the 2008 financial crisis and decimated by the Trump administration in early 2025, along with the US Justice Department, forced the bank to pay about $3 billion.[44] This sounds like a big win for good governance, but the cost of the settlement paled in comparison to the $15.7 billion the bank made in net profits over the twelve months before the settlement.[45] And that number does not account for the billions of dollars made by the bank during years of fraudulent activity.

Small community and regional banks cannot pay the cost of doing business relative to their larger competitors, so they are usually excluded from the core financial system. Inclusion, as defined by Acemoglu and Robinson, would provide a regulatory framework to even the playing field (e.g., design fair rules), allowing smaller banks to compete. However, the inequality caused by deregulation and porous regulatory frameworks is a system that will price out honest banks to the advantage of large banks. The cheaters win because they design the rules. All they need to do to stay in the game is pay the referee.

Economic inclusion does more than allow people to get good returns from their taxes. Inclusion also enables firms to actively and freely participate in economic exchanges. Unfortunately, American firms and small banks are being excluded as fast-growing big competitors crowd them out. The large firms operate by rules designed for their benefit. This lack of systemic inclusion increases inequality, eventually expanding the gaps between wealthy and poor households. Inequality is also endemic in markets and industries, pushing smaller firms further into the abyss while the largest rise.

Shortly after the 2008 financial collapse, Americans outside the privileged classes watched everyone fall into ruin as the bankers who caused the crash either suffered no real consequences or *benefited* from government bailouts. Americans concluded that the rule of law no longer applied to those at the top. Today, not much has changed. Small businesses and workers who try to make a living selling their ideas and labor on the market see the fruit of their work gobbled up by larger competitors and employers. The legal system and tax structure heavily favor the accumulation of capital controlled by large institutions. What can the poor and middle-class masses do when their government *designs* inequality?

To date, economic elites continue to operate within the framework of a democratic government. But what if those forms of government become inconvenient for elite power? How long will the wealthiest Americans, large corporations, banks, and firms—the sectors that benefit from deregulated markets—continue to tolerate a democratic system of governance? Acemoglu and Robinson say that when good governance and the rule of law are replaced with poor governance and naked corruption, a rich nation can quickly become a poor one.

The Danger of Polarization

If the United States is sliding away from good governance and the rule of law and into an abyss of poor governance and open corruption, as we believe, then when will economic malaise and frustrations explode into violence and conflict? Tolstoy observed in his classic book *Anna Karenina* that, "All happy families resemble each other, while every unhappy family is unhappy in its own way." This is true for nations that experience revolutions and civil wars, as compared to those that do not. A cynic might argue that an autocratic regime can buy civil order by providing "bread and circuses" to pacify the people. In modern parlance, we might say that the ruling class in the United States keeps people distracted with reality TV shows, online gambling, and social media feeds. But what types of situations can push a population into the streets to protest, and will that lead to violence?

Economist Debraj Ray of New York University proposes two measures: fractionalization and polarization. *Fractionalization* means the degree to which any given society contains diverse groups. *Polarization* occurs when two main groups are at odds. In Ray's studies, fractionalization—along ethnic, religious, economic, or cultural lines—showed no correlation with civil conflict. On the other hand, high degrees of polarization did show a significant correlation with civil conflict. In other words, diversity does not typically lead to violent conflict. However, polarization along highly unequal class divisions is highly associated with violent conflict.

Anecdotal evidence might seem to contradict this notion. Anyone who is vaguely aware of the long, sorry history of ethnic violence could name half a dozen violent conflicts that were motivated by a religious or ethnic differences. However, Ray claims that there is no *direct* effect, statistically speaking, of ethnic or religious fractionalization on the likelihood of civil conflict. Instead, Ray found that *per-capita income,* as measured in GDP US dollars, is a significant factor in the rise of conflict, both statistically and substantively.

Throughout this book we have emphasized the importance of per-capita GDP in American society. This does not mean that every poor country is primed to explode like a powder keg. Acemoglu and Robinson say that some economies are poor but inclusive, meaning there are lower levels of inequality and therefore less polarization. Ray points out that as income concentrates increasingly in the hands of one group, it polarizes the other group, which increases tensions in society. People who fall further from the GDP-per-capita line become more marginalized and therefore have less to lose during a conflict. They increasingly face an existential and desperate situation, so they become more willing to fight.

Ray, drawing on other research, emphasizes that economic polarization is not the only factor that can lead to social conflict. Another factor is the dispersion of economic and political power within a system. In a dispersed-power context, group loyalties remain localized; therefore, the demands of one group may be met or placated without injuring the interests of other groups. The framers of the US Constitution built a system of dispersed power, which Ray describes as federalism. In the not-so-distant past, laws and economic arrangements could vary significantly from state to state. For an example, before the 1980s banks were usually confined to a state or region. This restricted the ability of banks to consolidate wealth, and it hindered monopolistic tendencies in the provision of banking services. It also allowed smaller banks and credit unions to get a start and compete with their regional older siblings. After the deregulation of the 1980s, banks were allowed to compete across state lines and take advantage of increasing returns to scale; that is, they could decrease their average costs while increasing the number of services they provided. Like the Borg in *Star Trek: The Next Generation*, the banks were allowed to "assimilate" smaller banks—all the assets and networks—and move on to the next. Deregulation propelled the concentration of power within the banking system, destroying the dispersion that once kept it more versatile and diverse at a local or community level. Today, the banks continue to move away from a regulated federalism (dispersed power) to a more centralized system (concentrated power).

Ray contrasted federalism with a centralized system. The latter vests most political power in the hands of a few powerful leaders, which makes the society prone to polarization between the minority who hold and/or benefit from economic power and the majority who do not. When conflict occurs, the central authorities will find it hard to placate one group without antagonizing the other. When the 2008 Great Recession occurred, the large banks that were "too big to fail" received assistance from the Federal Reserve while smaller banks were left to die or be assimilated by larger banks. In the context of politics, the outsized importance of presidential races in modern America contributes to our nation's polarization.

Ray also describes the tension between "local compression" and "global compression" as another driver of civil conflict. His use of the terms *local* and *global* do not refer to physical geography; they refer to the distribution of income and wealth. People who experience *local compression* in an economic system cluster along specific segments of the income/wealth scale. In practical terms, this might mean that a nation has a large population of poor people, a small middle class, and an even smaller cluster of very wealthy people. As we mentioned earlier, about 50 percent of America's population takes home barely 10 percent of the nation's annual income, while the richest 20 percent take home about 50 percent of the nation's total income. By comparison, in a system with *global compression,* about 70 percent of the population is middle class. Only small populations—about 10 or 20 percent—live in the top and bottom quintiles.

In their 2011 survey of five thousand Americans, professors Michael Norton and William Arely asked respondents about their perceptions of wealth distribution in the United States. Then they asked respondents what they thought the distribution of wealth ought to be. In short, the survey showed that most Americans in 2011 understood that wealth distribution was moderately unequal, but they underestimated the severity of the nation's inequality. In addition, most people thought the nation ought to have a more equal distribution of wealth.[46]

This survey, while admittedly a bit out of date, shows that Americans live with a lot of cognitive dissonance about just how unequal America has become. Cognitive dissonance creates an inner tension that requires a response. This can lead to one of three outcomes. First, we could acknowledge the gravity of the problem and look for constructive solutions. This response is like a sick person who wisely seeks a diagnosis, listens to the doctor's recommended solution, and agrees to treatment. Second, we could recognize the problem but totally misdiagnose the cause or solution. This is like a sick person who recognizes the problem but then decides to trust an internet quack who sells snake oil rather than trust a doctor's scientific diagnosis and remedy. The third option is outright denial. This is like a person who recognizes the illness but decides to "party like it is 1999" with high quantities of alcohol in a night club. Why deal with a problem when you can ignore it *and* double down on it?

Cognitive dissonance on the individual level is complicated enough, but when it starts to affect a whole society, the responses can be, to put it mildly, messy. Societies that struggle with cognitive dissonance face one of the three choices described above, and two of them are counterproductive. American history reminds us that large populations once ignored the evils of slavery. This was not just an original sin of our nation, but a monumentally wrong decision in the face of collective cognitive dissonance. Except for our second President John Adams, who never owned a slave, the collective stance of the Founding Fathers was to look the other direction and hope the problem went away.[47] Thomas Jefferson even compared the institution of slavery to holding a wolf by the ears. "We can neither hold him, nor safely let him go. Justice on one scale, self-preservation on the other." This type of denial in the face of moral cognitive dissonance held for about a century, but as the evil of holding an entire ethnic group in bondage became too great to ignore, it produced all three of the reactions outlined above. Some people recognized the problem and proposed a solution, the obvious choice being abolition. Other people recognized the problem but could not bring themselves to embrace racial equality. These people opted for the Free Soil movement. They feared that slavery would be a threat to them and their communities, so they sought legal barriers to keep the practice out of their states. A third group refused to acknowledge that slavery was a problem. For them, the obvious solution came in the form of secession.

For as long as the Southern plantation owners believed the federal government would leave their property—the slaves—alone, they continued to participate in building the United States during the first half of the nineteenth century. At that time, the system of authority was highly federalized (dispersed), and the degrees of economic compression were much more influenced by each state's economic model. But as Southern plantation owners tried to enforce runaway slave laws on Northern states, they began to antagonize the Northerners. Eventually this antagonism led to the demise of the

Whig party and the formation of the Republican party.

President Abraham Lincoln did not vow to end slavery in the South, but he did oppose the spread of slavery to the West. He also called for an end to the enforcement of runaway slave laws, which conflicted with state laws in the North. These actions led Southern plantation owners to assume that abolition would follow as soon as enough Western Free States entered the union. As the federal government threatened the interests of Southern plantation owners, they increasingly moved toward secession. Some apologists for the Confederacy say the South simply wanted to be left alone; however, runaway slave laws, enforced by either private slavecatchers or federal marshals, contradicted the spirit of federalism (dispersing power to the states). This made the conflict as much about central authority as it was about economics and the moral treatment of human beings.

Our purpose in this discussion is to illustrate that the collective responses leading to the US Civil War played a significant role in the violence. The war killed about 620,000 soldiers, plus an estimated fifty thousand civilians. Up to ten thousand more people died during the Reconstruction Era from 1865 to 1876.

The past can often serve as a guide to the future. Our situation today is fundamentally different in most regards, but it is important to recognize the role of cognitive dissonance in the way Americans perceive and respond to today's economic inequality.

Paths for People

In what ways can individuals respond to a system that is so wildly and obviously designed against them? The easy answers involve building social networks and communities outside the control of employers and politicians. However, that might not be sufficient. If we are in a lifeboat taking on water and we have no buckets to bail it out, what should we do? Use our hands? Jump overboard and pray for the best? In the *Lord of the Rings,* King Theoden might look at the massive waves of inequality inherent in our system and ask, "What can men do against such reckless hate?" Likewise, what can we Hobbits do against the powerful forces of "natural monopolies"? Wealthy households enjoy playing by rules designed for their advantage.

As isolated individuals, Americans have little hope of changing the macroeconomic forces that negatively impact us. No one can deal with such a situation alone. The riptide that threatens to drag us farther out to sea is too strong. Somehow we need to form citizen alliances. The work of Debraj Ray shows that a diverse society and pluralism is not a problem. The danger is polarization. This implies that Americans must find ways to bind together. If we are divided, we will not stand.

Forge Local Connections

We recommend forming connections at a local level. That is where we can get to know people, find ways to serve in tangible ways, hold face-to-face discussions, and engage in small associations.

It will take the work of sizeable, diverse groups comprising people from lower, middle, and upper-middle classes. The goal and strategy should be clear and simple.

First, these associations should work relentlessly to pressure elected officials at the state and federal levels to change the design of our economy. Pick one issue and work exclusively on that. Having a specific focus will prevent the group from feeling overwhelmed by all the needs in the world. One example would be the hugely popular idea of "Medicare for All," which would provide universal health insurance for all Americans. Health care expenses wipe out thousands of families every year while insurance companies look for ways to *not cover people in need.* Study the topic thoroughly, formulate a message that is based on research and strong arguments, and then work together to push for change. Find other groups working on the same issue and team up with them. Perhaps you can identify a different issue that is more related to your local situation, but you get the idea.

Second, consumers have a lot of power that we never use. Why do Jeff Bezos, Mark Zuckerberg, and the AI tech bosses have so much power? *Because we buy their products and services.* We give them our money. Small businesses spend advertising dollars on big social media platforms instead of finding alternative ways to sell products and services. We read news (often unverified) on social media platforms for free rather than paying for subscriptions to serious local and national newspapers and magazines. We order socks from Amazon rather than going to a local sock shop. So, imagine what might happen if millions of Americans decided to stop sending money to the billionaires who run companies that have more wealth than most countries in the world? We consumers usually make purchasing decisions based on speed, cost, and efficiency. That is understandable, because we are broke, busy, and tired. But there are ways to change our consumer choices without adding significant financial and time costs. Here is a story that illustrates what we mean.

In April 2025, on a weekend designated to commemorate small independent bookstores, Amazon launched a massive online book sale, cutting the prices of books by up to 65 percent. By doing this, the company tried to undercut book sales at local stores and on non-Amazon sites for books. In addition, Amazon's price reductions reduced profits for publishers and authors. During that weekend, our publisher put the word out to buy books from any company other than Amazon: go to a nearby bookstore, or buy online from Barnes and Noble or Bookshop.org. Our publisher argued that, for example, Bookshop.org is a B-Corp company that donates a percentage of sales (a total of $38 million as of April 2025) to local independent bookstores. Rather than seeking to wipe out competition, Bookshop.org seeks to support communities by supporting local physical bookstores. A friend of our publisher responded to his suggestion by saying, "Yeah, but Amazon prices are cheaper, the shipping is free, and the book will arrive overnight." See how we are primed (pardon the pun) to succumb to whatever is easy, fast, and cheap—even if it means our purchases help multibillionaires take joyrides in space? As consumers, we can (and should) do more to think about where we spend our money. We can do a lot to defund the oligarchs.

We admit that the ideas presented above are mere sketches. Many readers will look for a specific plan and detailed strategy. But we, the authors, do not have all the answers. So, we encourage you to start a conversation with a few friends, talk about the needs, and generate a few feasible plans. This book could be a catalyst for that initial conversation. How about a book club that centers on the topics and subtopics in this book? Tall trees grow from small seeds.

Paths for Policy

Most debates about economic policy leave morality out of the conversation. When the discussions center on growth rates and quarterly earnings reports, all the ones and zeros suppress questions about moral principles. As a result, we allow the nihilism of rapacious greed to triumph.

How can we begin a conversation about moral economic principles? Most average Americans believe that the economy should be run in alignment with a moral-philosophical worldview, but what system of ethical economics could we—a society of more than 330 million citizens—hope to agree on? Re-regulation? Massive redistribution of wealth? Those ideas are unlikely starting points because they are disconnected from broader, foundational philosophical questions. Nevertheless, we know that there are other systems of economic theory beyond America's current neoliberal model. We present three ideas here. They are not the only alternatives.

Our first proposed theory of political economy is called *distributism*. Race Mathews, an Austrian economist, argued that the right to property was fundamental. His theories found an enthusiastic patron in the Catholic Church. The underlying idea of distributism is that spreading economic power as widely and deeply as practicable will inoculate a society against kleptocracy and oligarchic control. By transferring economically productive assets to a broad population, and by setting up guilds (like an association) to enforce standards and ethics, distributism can theoretically provide an egalitarian economic order and a cohesive social order. Contemporary political parties like the Christian Democrats in Bavaria, for example, favor such an economic model.

A second political-economic theory is called *cooperatism*. This theory advocates for the workers' and business cooperatives that we discussed earlier in the book. By giving economic control to the people who work on the shop floors and offices of an industry, companies give employees a share of the profits and a stake in the future of a profit-making enterprise. Setting up co-ops that link customers as directly as possible with producers, while marginalizing the intermediaries and rent-seekers, benefits both the producer and the purchaser. Originally referred to as *syndicalism* in the early twentieth century, this theory does not require a new or complicated framework for a whole society; it just requires that people be as directly tied to the outcomes of their economic decisions as possible. The goal is to give people more agency in the economy, which is sorely lacking in America today.

The third economic model could be implemented tomorrow if the Federal Reserve would accede to it. This theory is called *social credit*. It advocates turning the banking system into a public utility. Rather than functioning as a for-profit industry, the monetary system would lend capital directly to citizens at the basement-level interest rates that only the banking sector now enjoys. By giving large banks discount interest rates, the government is subsidizing the banks, which is an example of "corporate socialism." The rules are unfair to everyone else. Under the social credit model, savings would be managed by credit unions or directly by the monetary institution. For further reading, check out the writings of C.H. Douglas who lived through the Great Depression and thought, "Are we really just running an economy to benefit a few bankers?"

CHAPTER 9

Historical Maladies

No matter how bad one thinks economic inequality might be in the US, it is much worse. The primary driver is naked self-interest. Without meaningful change, the economy could become even more unequal. The pressures could keep building up. Frustration and polarization could continue to be met with the aristocracy's inflexibility. Eventually, dams with too much pressure crack and collapse. If that happens, then what?

Hopefully, that will *not* happen. That is why we wrote this book. We hope that good solutions will be enacted. We hope that everyone will work together to relieve the crushing inequality that is so prevalent in America today. We hope that legal and economic reforms might reduce the pressure behind the dam. The ideas discussed in the previous chapters might give average people enough reason to believe the system can still work. If that can be achieved, then it becomes much easier for people to turn their backs on extremist demagogues who want supreme authority.

But what happens if the dam breaks? To answer that question, we can learn some lessons from history. What happened in the past is not guaranteed to happen in the future; however, this chapter provides examples of how inequality has played out in history.

Taiping Rebellion, 1850 to 1864

The Taiping Rebellion in China, occurring from 1850 to 1864, resulted in the triumph of Qing Dynasty forces over those fighting under the banner of the Heavenly Kingdom Movement. Broadly speaking, the rebels sought to overthrow the Qing Dynasty because it had lost the Mandate of Heaven, a concept analogous to the Divine Right in the West. The backdrop of this revolution included military defeats by foreign powers, famines caused by natural disasters, heavy taxation of the peasantry, and an increasingly corrupt centralized bureaucracy. To say China under the Qing Dynasty was a highly unequal society would be an understatement.

The forces of the dynasty defeated the rebel movements, at the cost of at least twenty million to thirty million people and the vast devastation of central China. Some historians say as many as one hundred million people died. Even if the lower range is more accurate, that number of casualties would not count injuries, displacement, and long-term impoverishment. China's pre-rebellion population was about 430 million. It did not increase until the 1920s, after the establishment of the Republic of China in 1911-1912. This suggests that the demographic consequences of the Taiping Rebellion impacted the country for generations. In the end, the dynasty staggered to a final inglorious end at the hands of Westernizing republicans and opportunistic warlords.

What lessons might we draw from nineteenth century Chinese history? Prior to the rebellion, the Qing Dynasty suffered from underlying economic fragilities as China spent fifty years frittering away its economic strengths. The dynasty also faced external pressures, such as when the United Kingdom's superior warships forced China to open its ports and domestic markets to cheaper European goods and opium from British India. The Chinese production of luxury goods like silk and porcelain eroded, further degrading the Chinese economy. Chinese agricultural techniques had difficulty keeping up with the growing population. Autocratic governance imposed intellectual stagnation. Bureaucracies resorted to bribery and petty infighting to influence the emperor's decisions.

By 1850, the country could not even feed its own population. As the social "dam" collapsed, the idea of rebellion fomented into actual rebellion. In response to that, the dynasty increasingly chose to use brute force against its own citizens rather than humbly cooperate.

Irish Potato Famine, 1845 to 1852

Another example shows how the extreme concentration of economic activity can lead to humanitarian disasters rather than revolution. It was called the Irish Potato Famine (1845-1852). How did this famine occur? For centuries prior to the crisis, English and Scottish plantation owners bought, seized, or stole most of the good agricultural land in Ireland. That practice was fueled by the introduction of the potato from the Americas. The potato provided a nutritious staple crop that was easy to grow. By the early eighteenth century, over a hundred varieties of potatoes grew on subsistence farms across the island.

By 1840, five years before the famine started, almost a fifth of the Emerald Isle's rural population lived in poverty, with many people working as itinerant laborers. This was a downstream effect of the consolidation of wealth and property that had occurred during the previous centuries. Lacking their own land, the itinerant workers could only farm the most marginal land to feed themselves while trying to eke out a living.

Another factor that set the stage for all-out famine was the gradual loss of diverse potato varieties. By 1840, just five years before the famine hit, farmers grew only four varieties of potatoes. Then wet weather combined with the arrival of a fungal blight. Between a quarter and a third of the potato crop failed. Malnutrition and starvation quickly followed.

The English made a bad situation much, much worse. The British had ample grain stores. They probably could have prevented the deaths of thousands and thousands of Irish people during the seven-year famine. However, the prime minister, who had begun some belated relief efforts, lost a no-confidence vote in Parliament. His replacement believed in free-market fundamentalism and refused to authorize further grain shipments for fear it would distort the market. He also believed that the Irish needed to be taught a civics lesson about self-reliance. By starving.

The story shows, again, how the concentration of economic power can exert a push-pull effect. Many Irish who might have survived the famine on small holdings could not do so because all the good land had been taken by the English and Scottish plantation owners. This forced the Irish farmers to depend on one crop. Then the varieties of that crop dwindled to just four. All redundancy and resilience in the system had been removed for the purpose of concentrating wealth and increasing efficiency. This worked out fine until it no longer did. When relief could have come from the upper classes who controlled the grain supply, a simple decision in London to teach the Irish a lesson in self-reliance led to a humanitarian disaster. Fortunately (if you can call it that), the Irish had an avenue of escape: emigration, principally to the United States.

The French Revolution, 1789

Our next historical example involves powdered wigs, fancy pants, and a society wracked by economic and political inequality: France, 1789, home to the mother of all modern revolutions.

The Bourbons, the royal family who presided over France on the eve of the French Revolution, ruled a country with income distributions shockingly similar to the current income distribution of the United States. The system of taxation in *ancien regime* France contained many loopholes and wild variations across regions and classes, so tax records do not provide a 100 percent accurate proxy for income. That makes it problematic for historians to estimate incomes. The records that survived the revolution vary in quality and completeness, so any modern estimates need to come with a healthy helping of salt.

Speaking of salt, everyone in France except the nobility and clergy had to pay a salt tax. In some regions, the rate was ruinously high for people who ran small farms. The economy of eighteenth-century France was overwhelmingly agricultural. Only 20 percent of the population lived in towns or cities with more than two thousand people. The other 80 percent lived in rural areas. The average population of a village, hamlet, or parish was six hundred. Those who lived in larger cities like Paris and Lyon worked as artisans, shopkeepers, and day laborers. They did not work in large factories because the Industrial Revolution did not really have an impact until the mid-nineteenth century. France did operate under an absolute monarchy leading up to the revolution, but the power of French kings, however autocratic it looks to us today, did not enjoy the sweeping powers of the monarchs in Central and Eastern Europe. The king's inability to raise new taxes without the consent of the nobility lit the fuse that led to the revolution.

Many modern ideas of government and law, including in the US, spring directly from the tumultuous years from 1789 to 1793. During that era, people sought answers to questions about the rights of citizens and who can be classified as a citizen. The distinction between the passive and active citizen hinged on how much each person paid in taxes. This idea still finds its way into public discourse today when we discuss "takers" and "makers."

For all the differences between France then and the US now, some quantitative similarities stand out. First, the tax code of Bourbon France rivals in complexity with the US tax code today. Every group—nobility, the church, towns, and provinces—each managed to carve out exemptions for themselves while shifting tax burdens onto anyone who did not have the legal authority to push back against those taxes. In the US today, billionaires lobby Congress to win lower tax rates, for example by protecting 15 percent capital gains rates. Large corporations sometimes receive so many tax credits that the government *pays them* on April 15.

Second, France in the eighteenth century operated one of the largest and most effective militaries in Europe. France's military did not win every war they fought, but when the French army and navy went toe-to-toe with England, Austria, and Prussia, they often emerged victorious. It is reasonable to say that the French military's battlefield victories were offset by the monarchy's diplomatic losses. French aid played a crucial role in helping Americans win their revolution against England, but the monarchy racked up debts without providing the French people with many benefits. These negative outcomes (for France) immediately preceded the French Revolution. Today, the United States has a gargantuan defense budget. Battlefield results have been mixed. When it comes to "winning the peace," the geopolitical and fiscal situation of late eighteenth-century France strongly resembles the US situation today.

Third, there is a striking similarity between today's inequality in the US and the inequality in pre-revolution France. As a reminder, estimates of income inequality in eighteenth-century France are the product of incomplete records and proxy measures. As a result, our estimates derive from three core methods: inferences from the capitation tax; analysis of known socio-professional structures; and an eighteenth-century effort to quantify the economic structure of the kingdom. For our purposes, we draw heavily on the paper titled "The Income Inequality of France in Historical Perspective" by Christian Morrison and Wayne Snyder.[48] This study represents some of the most thorough, scholarly work on the subject. The researchers produced an estimate of income inequality in eighteenth-century France that is remarkably similar to the contours of income inequality in modern America. Income distributions for each income group in France comes from Morrison and Snyder. The US numbers come from the Cato Institute's adjusted gross income report cited earlier in this book.

Income Group	18th Century France	21st Century USA
Top 10% (Top Decile)	47-53%	52%
Top 11-30%	21-23%	23%
Bottom 70%	26-30%	24%

Figure 9-1: Comparison of income inequality, as a percentage of wealth owned by each economic group, in eighteenth-century France and twenty-first century United States.

In both cases, these estimates likely underestimate actual economic inequality because annual income does not measure accumulated wealth or certain groups' broader power and influence within society. A lowly French peasant would never even dream of influencing state policy by, for instance, asking for an exemption from the salt tax. The numbers above show a dire situation, but the reality was (and is) much worse. The similarities between France in the past and the US in the present should give us a sense of foreboding about our future.

No single factor caused the French Revolution, but economic inequality, as experienced by the starving urban day laborers of Paris and the subsistence farmers, was a powerful driver of the events in 1789 France and afterward. Warning bells preceded the pivotal revolution, which lasted until 1793. The most notable included the numerous bread riots in 1775, which historians refer to as the Flour Wars. The semi-cohesive demands of the impoverished French people indicated a growing realization that the highly unequal system of the *ancien regime* was potentially lethal. The level of inequality in

France, as shown in figure 9-1, was less than what the US faces today, but poverty was killing the French. The royal government prevailed in the Flour Wars, but these uprisings left little doubt in the minds of the poor that the government would rather see them starve or die by bayonet than offer substantial assistance. In modern America, what form might equivalent events take? Over the last decade or two, state power has crushed protest movements of all stripes. When the tear gas clears, citizens are left to wonder if peaceful reform is even possible. Have our precursory Flour Wars already occurred?

Romanov Russia, 1905 to 1917

Economic inequality and the near starvation of a population do not alone a revolution make. Even when an economic and political system operates wildly out of balance, it sometimes takes an outside event to shock a system toward reform. And when reforms do not go far enough, citizens often start asking questions about the prevailing regime—questions like, Why do the Romanovs rule Russia in the first place? Do we need a tsar at all?

One common answer in 1905 Russia (and in certain circles today) was: "God appointed the tsar." In the early 1600s, the Romanov family fought for and gained control of Muscovy. They had expanded and ruled the state that came to be called the Russian Empire. You cannot pull that off without divine favor, right? Well, the history is far more complex and messier than our pithy description above. The Romanov family's right to rule did not come from God, but from the benevolent father-tsar who extended protection to his children and all peoples who lived in the Russian

Empire. Martial prowess was one pillar of tsarist rule. Another was the imposition of the Orthodox Church as the state religion. The third pillar comprised nobles who cut deals to govern locally on behalf of the tsars. The success of the Russian army in conquering about one-sixth of all land in the world went a long way, in the minds of many, to justify the existence of the tsarist state.

By 1904, the twin forces of increasingly globalized credit, which floated the value of the ruble, and industrialization, which drew ever-increasing numbers of people from the empire's countryside to the cities, shifted the balance of economic power away from the landed nobility and toward the urban workers and the rising class of professionals and capitalists. As of 1900, French banks invested (loaned) roughly $4.1 billion (in 1990 dollars) in the Russian economy. In 1914, they invested another $4.7 billion. These amounts do not seem like much today, but the loans built factories and railroads, and they provided funds to the tsarist state. The investments increased the value of the ruble on international financial markets, which made imports cheaper. The funds also allowed the Russian Empire to increase agricultural and industrial output, making Russian exports cheaper on the international market. This made the process of industrialization easier for the empire, but it made the process more volatile for working and professional classes. As cities endured sweeping changes, economic growth did not occur in rural areas. The institutions of common landholdings by peasant communes, who represented at least 80 percent of the population, probably limited the growing economic inequality in the Russian countryside. But in the cities, people worked twelve hours a day, six days a week with dismally low wages and atrocious living conditions.

We can compare the inequality of Russia in 1904 with the US inequality in 2023. According to the US Census Bureau, the top 1 percent of Americans in 2023 had 21.1 percent of all income and the bottom 40 percent of Americans had 13.1 percent of all income. In 1904 Russia, the top 1 percent of Russians had 13.5 percent of all income and the bottom 40 percent had 21.3 percent.[49] These numbers do not give us an exact apples-to-apples comparison, but we can see that US income inequality in 2023 was worse than Russia's inequality in 1904. In the US, the top 1 percent of Americans had a higher share of income than the wealthiest 1 percent of Russians in 1904. Moreover, the poorest Americans had a lower percentage of income in 2023 than the poorest Russians had prior to the 1905 Revolution.

In this economic context, Russia ended up in the Russo-Japanese War (1904 to 1905). Russia's foreign trade balance made the consequences of military defeat much more dire. The Romanovs did not start the war, but they also did not end it on their own terms. After a string of crushing defeats, including the annihilation of the Baltic Fleet at the Battle of Tsushima, and the destruction of two armies in Manchuria, the Romanovs threw in the towel and agreed to arbitration by the United States.

The war intersected with Russia's economy in a decisive way. The defeats in Asia collapsed the value of the ruble; about twenty-three million rubles in foreign investment flowed out of the country in the immediate aftermath of Russia's defeat. This financial loss was not that large in comparison to the whole Russian economy, but the effects fell disproportionately on working class people in large cities. Employment became harder to find or maintain, while the cost of everything linked to foreign markets rose.

In response to worsening economic conditions, the workers of St. Petersburg marched on the Winter Palace, begging their metaphorical father (the "good tsar") to intervene on their behalf. Instead, the tsar's troops opened fire, killing an estimated thirteen hundred people. That was the spark. Over the next year and a half, between peasant revolts, industrial strikes, and even some army mutinies, the regime appeared to be bound for total collapse. Only belated reforms and a new constitution quelled the chaos. However, from 1906 to about 1912 the reforms faltered, giving way to autocratic backsliding. That destroyed what remained of the Romanov dynasty's credibility, setting the stage for the eventual overthrow of the tsar in February 1917.

The revolution of 1904 could be compared to the Flour Wars that preceded the 1789 revolution in France—as a warning sign. However, the real issue was that Russia's loss in the Russo-Japanese War diminished the country's perceived invincibility. Russia had a larger economy, population, and military, so the loss struck the heart of the Romanov's legitimacy to rule the Russian Empire.

America's military today gobbles up 52 percent of the federal government's annual discretionary budget, which is why the US has the best-funded military in the world. This air of military invincibility, coupled with the dollar's place as the world's reserve currency, depresses the prices of imported raw materials and manufactured goods for American consumers and businesses. But a military defeat abroad could easily produce effects like those seen in Russia in 1904 to 1905, driving up the costs of imports and the cost of US debt. Could the federal government survive challenges like those?

Mexico's Porfiriato Period, 1910 to 1920

What happens when an economy is changing rapidly, when new technologies constantly revolutionize commerce and industry, and when the government is controlled by technocratic elites who do not care about the impact of their decisions on the population? In the case of Mexico, the result was a violent revolution, a series of coups and countercoups, several foreign interventions, and at least a decade of civil war.

A man named Porfirio Diaz took control of the Mexican government in 1876. He ruled the country until his ouster in 1910. During that time, he and his government transformed Mexico from an impoverished agrarian nation that had been defeated by the United States in 1848 to 1849 into an industrializing, rising economic power. The emergence of a working class occurred in the cities, mines, and oilfields. Simultaneously, an economically powerful middle class emerged in Mexico City. This inequality created a potent combination of economic and intellectual dissatisfaction with the existing order.

Just before the 1910 election, which was democratic in name only, Diaz publicly stated that he would not run again. At eighty years old, this made sense to the people of Mexico; Diaz would retire in comfort and make way for the next generation. But Diaz changed his mind and ran again for election. Not a good decision. He was ousted. The situation did not improve. His successor, Francisco Madero, could not pacify the population. After a period of instability and infighting, the 1914 Ten Tragic Days erupted. Army General Victoriano Huerta overthrew the Madero government, kicking off the bloodiest period of fighting, which lasted until 1920.

The Diaz regime failed in part because his entire ruling clique consisted of men in their seventies and eighties. All of them were friends and allies of Diaz. This cadre managed to stay in power through decades of instability and liberal economic reforms, but their ideas and legitimacy persisted beyond the expiration date. Younger men and women wanted to see new political and economic leaders, which they thought they would get in 1910. When Diaz sought power again and failed, the installation of Francisco Madero did not resolve the underlying angst of the Mexicans. Civil war was the outcome.

Inequality initially declined in Mexico in the 1920s and 1930s, in part because of the leveling effect of the civil war. Land reforms and the increased power of industrial unions also reduced inequality. The legitimacy of the new government rested to some degree on honoring economic and political concessions extracted during the war-torn 1910s. Mexico's Gini coefficient, a statistical measure of inequality, dropped from 0.46 in 1910 to 0.41 by 1930. Unfortunately for the Mexican people, high degrees of economic inequality returned by 1940; the Gini coefficient rose to 0.51.

This summary of the Mexican Revolution and its aftermath in the 1920s is a simplification of all that happened. The moral of the story is that when the leadership of a rapidly changing country remains in the hands of a gerontocracy at the expense of younger generations, the leaders face intense scrutiny. The question morphs from, "Why can't new people run the place?" to, "Why can't some new ideas run the place" to, "Maybe we need a whole new way to run the place."

The incorporation of new technologies, such as the railroad

and telegraph, during the Porfiriato period increased incomes for the rich. Train systems connected urban elites with each other while decreasing the connections between rural communities who could not afford to ride trains. Rail systems did help move rural and farm goods to market quicker, but the real money was made by railroad owners and mercantile exchanges who sold those goods after they arrived at train stations.

In the US, the incorporation of modern technologies in the late 1990s and early 2000s led to a quick decrease in the Gini coefficient (a reduction of inequality). That did not last long. As the US advanced the tech boom, the Gini coefficient showed a sustained increase. The Great Recession and the Covid-19 pandemic had some leveling effects, because each destroyed massive amounts of wealth. But as soon as the nation rebounded from those crises, inequality continued to increase.

As stated earlier, technology will not save us from inequality just as it did not save Mexico during the Porfiriato period. Trains and telegraphs revolutionized the economy of Mexico, but those advances left the rural poor at the station. The tech boom in the US appears to have had a similar effect; anyone today can surf the web from a smartphone, but the companies that make phones and computers are the only ones making real money. Will the rise of artificial intelligence reduce inequality or increase it? That depends on how AI company leaders and policymakers *choose to design and regulate* the use of these technologies. We will soon discover the answer.

The Future of America's Professional Managerial Class

We Americans might think that history's revolutions do not apply to us. After all, those past examples consisted of agrarian, rural societies rooted in traditional ways of life. We think that assumption is incorrect. The people in those historical instances felt compelled to act for universally human reasons. When people struggle to get by, and when they see that the rules of the game only benefit those at the top of the heap, they cannot help but become frustrated. That frustration metastasizes into a resolve to treat the state and the ruling class as they have been treated. Do we think that human nature is different today?

Today, the US has a large population of what we call the professional-managerial class (PMC). It is reasonable to argue that Weimar Germany, or the final years of the Soviet Union, closely resemble PMC America. Both Germany in the 1920s and the Soviet Union in the 1980s were heavily urbanized, industrial societies with literate, mostly secular populations. However, the Weimar Republic never enjoyed popular legitimacy. Beyond Berlin's liberal intelligentsia, the rest of the population believed that the republic was controlled by effete (self-indulgent) liberals who had stabbed Germany in the back to end the First World War. The fact that the Weimar Republic still lasted about twelve years after the war seems remarkable in hindsight. For Germans at the time, it seemed reasonable to toss out the government. Unfortunately, they got something much worse after 1933, and it involved swastikas.

Whereas the Third Reich dramatically overthrew the Weimar

Republic, the Soviet Union died mostly peacefully at home. From 1917 to 1991, the Union of Soviet Socialist Republics staked its entire authority on being better at delivering the goods than the tsars and the capitalists. That did not work out. Dictators struggle to argue that they have built a prosperous, workers' paradise when everyone is standing in bread lines and secret police officers lurk everywhere.

For reasons related to collective psychology, the older examples we described above are highly relevant for us today. The Romanovs ruled Russia (among other places) from 1613 to 1917. The Bourbons ruled France from 1589 to 1793 and then again under the restored Bourbons from 1815-1848. Diaz ruled Mexico from 1876 to 1910, but Mexico had been independent since 1820. The point is this: The people who lived during these overthrown regimes would not have known any other type of political economy than the one in which they lived.

In this sense, the United States is ancient. If we start at the inauguration of George Washington in 1791, the US Constitution has been the operating document of government for 234 years (as of 2025). Bad presidents come and go. Our history is not only a story of sunshine, roses, and puppy dogs, but the law of the land remains the same. Historians William Stauss and Neil Howe point out that the US has endured a complete overturning of the ruling consensus three times.[50] In 1783, local aristocrats replaced distant ones after the American Revolution. Then in 1865, industrial magnates replaced landed aristocrats. And in 1933, the managerial class replaced the industrialists as America's leadership class. We (the authors) do not put full stock in this view of US history, but the pattern of cyclical overturning every eighty or one hundred years seems evident.

Economic chaos preceded two of these massive changes: the Panic of 1857 and the 1929 Stock Market Crash. The thirteen colonies were not terribly unequal or impoverished, but the British Parliament in 1763 to 1775 passed a series of acts that disrupted trade between the colonies and the wider world just before the American Revolution. Stark economic indicators preceded all these tumultuous events. It is reasonable to think that our current political economy might be a dam about to crack.

Levels of US income inequality rival that of late-Bourbon France. Opulence and decadence by the few existed in the clouds above the crushing poverty of the many. The people who governed France seemed genuinely oblivious to the suffering below. In Russia, due to the strong value of the ruble, Russians in the early twentieth-century benefited immensely from cheap French loans. Today, the American dollar is the world's reserve currency due to post-World War II international banking systems. This alone makes imports cheaper for Americans, giving a boost to households who purchase artificially cheaper foreign goods. Upsetting that system of finance and trade, which could happen as we write in the spring of 2025 or because of a stinging military defeat, could result in a crisis that is more disastrous than the 2008 Great Recession.

Other similarities between historical examples and the US today are aplenty. As with Mexico in 1910, an elderly man has occupied the Oval Office since early 2017. Americans, for some reason, think these elderly men can make decisions about a technologically dynamic economy they barely understand. The average age of a US senator is sixty-five, which means that half the Senate is past retirement age. By comparison, with an average age of fifty-seven, the House of Representatives looks spry. We do not seek to disparage the wisdom of the elders, but it cannot bode well that the people writing federal laws acquired their worldview sometime around 1980 or earlier. As with Diaz in 1910, old men who contest elections they clearly lost often make decisions that put younger people's lives in the line of fire.

In these types of political-economic environments, especially when autocracy settles in, corruption increases. Some congressional representatives, knowing that this decision or that decision is going to happen, are famous for making prescient and personally beneficial investments. Most normal people would call this insider trading, but those in Congress see it as the warm glow of being around the wise financial advice of in-the-know peers. Why would they change the system that benefits them?

In 1789, 1904, and 1910, there was no shortage of fringe groups who hawked conspiracy theories and proffered untested ideas about how to reform their respective societies. Some of those groups were marginalized and others came within reach of the power centers. Similarly, America is full of elite groups chomping at the bit to "be the change" they want to see in the world. For example, a deep-pocketed techno-aristocracy subscribes to an autocratic worldview, one in which they make the decisions. This worldview is often called a technocracy.[51] In the view of men like Peter Theil and Curtis Yarvin, a system of neo-feudal technocracy should replace the flailing PMC meritocracy. These men have no time for the compromises required in a democracy. In the spring of 2025, some of them seem to have little regard for the rule of law. That should not be surprising; they come from a corporate culture that believes the mantra "move fast and break stuff." What a time to be alive.

CHAPTER 10

Something Wicked This Way Comes

In about 1980, the main drivers of US economic gains began to shift away from manufacturing and small businesses. The profitability of large companies increased with every tax cut and deregulatory action. Those fat profits did not trickle down to the rest of us; instead, they flowed up to financial institutions and the ultra-rich. During the 1990s, this trend accelerated as corporate leaders offshored jobs and as computers and robotics made other jobs redundant. Thanks to economies of scale, these trends allowed larger companies to gobble up smaller, domestic competitors. By 2010, global supply chains continued to erode US manufacturing, e-commerce (e.g., Amazon) began to bankrupt small-scale retail businesses, and "too big to fail" policies were set up to insure large financial institutions. Education, the traditional path to a middle-class income, costs more but does not produce the same benefits that previous generations enjoyed. To put it mildly, the political economy of the United States in 2024 looks quite different and worse than it did fifty years ago.

Today, lawmakers in Washington only see one direction for the country to go: more of the same. About 80 percent of the savings from the Tax Cuts and Jobs Act of 2017—the Trump tax cuts—are projected to go to the top 1 percent of earners from 2017-2027. The social safety net programs, stimulus checks, child tax credits, and the temporary moratorium on student loan payments during the Covid-19 pandemic temporarily flattened inequality during the Covid-19 recession, but those efforts did nothing to solve underlying problems. Since 2021, the pre-pandemic trends returned to their baselines, pushing more wealth into fewer and fewer hands.

As this book goes to press in June 2025, Congress is considering additional tax cuts that would benefit primarily the top 10 percent of Americans. The nonpartisan Congressional Budget Office released an analysis on a bill that cuts taxes and cuts spending on safety-net programs like Medicaid and food stamps. If the bill passes, the bottom 10 percent of Americans would lose government benefits worth an average of $1,559 each year over the next decade, or a total average loss of about $16,000. By comparison, the top 10 percent of Americans would see a 2.3 percent annual income gain, or an average of $12,044 per year until 2034. The total gain for wealthy Americans on average over ten years would be more than $120,000.[52]

To make matters worse for poorer Americans, the version of the legislation that passed the House removes health coverage from nearly eleven million Americans. Without health insurance, many will not be able to afford care when they are injured or sick, which means it will be harder for them to work. For those who can afford to pay one medical bill out of pocket, the astronomical fee could lead to bankruptcy. Worse still, the CBO estimates that the bill will add nearly $3 trillion to the debt over the next decade.[53] This debt burden will be passed down to our children and grandchildren. Is that moral? Is that even a traditional "conservative" value? No matter how bad you think economic inequality is in the US, it is likely to get even worse.

As Republicans in Congress continue to promote tax cuts that benefit the wealthiest Americans, they do so while promoting an old and nefarious myth: "trickledown economics." Many wealthy proponents of this myth say that implementing tax-cut policies will be better for the lower classes because, by reducing taxes those with capital will reinvest their wealth productively into the economy, thereby increasing the size of the economic pie.

We all agree that the economic pie can grow and that all people, theoretically, can benefit together from that growth. However, what happens if wealthy Americans and corporations keep the tax cuts and do not reinvest the capital into the economy? The funneling of wealth to an ever-shrinking number of people, combined with higher interest rates and a tighter money supply, turns the economy into a zero-sum game. The wealthiest individuals and large corporations gobble up all the new growth. Every dollar vacuumed up by the ultra-rich does not go back into the sectors of the economy that benefit average households and workers. This is why 1 percent of Americans hold 23 percent of all household net wealth, which is the same amount of wealth held by the *entire middle 60 percent* of the population by income. It is worth saying again: 3.3 million Americans have more wealth than 247 million Americans combined. As a result of their massive wealth, they can (and do) exercise outsized influence over markets and the government. These people own controlling stakes in all major US corporations and both political parties.

Why has this happened? Those at the top of the economy often say that the problem lies with the moral and/or intellectual failings of the lower classes. A common mantra is, If you work hard and play by the rules, every person can attain the American dream. That idea stems from the 1950s when the rules were fairer to hard-working families. Today, the rules are designed to subsidize and protect the wealthy. So, even when average Americans "play by the rules," they are playing a game that is rigged to benefit wealthy Americans. Any misconception that inequality stems from the moral failings or laziness of the poor and soon-to-be poor should be put in the garbage dump. In this economy, hard work and gumption often do not allow people to get ahead.

Every year, this situation pushes the political culture of the nation closer to the breaking point. Political candidates almost all come from the top 10 percent income bracket, and most of them share the worldview of the top 1 percent. Recent research by the Center for Responsive Politics found that about 52 percent of Congresspeople have a net worth of over $1 million. Politicians receive a flood of money from those who can spare a few million every two or four years, which effectively drowns out the voices of average voters. The flood of money to political parties and super-PACs certainly creates "a rising tide," but it only lifts the boats (yachts?) of those who adhere to the ideology of the richest Americans.

In 2022, the average amount spent to win a seat in the House of Representatives was about $2.8 million. Senate seats cost about ten times more, averaging a whopping $26.5 million. By comparison, in 1990 a winning campaign cost $950,000 for a House seat and $3.87 million for a Senate seat. (Those numbers are adjusted for inflation). Today, the money comes primarily from the top 10 percent of income earners. Indeed, these numbers suggest that economic inequality grew just as fast in Congress as it did across the nation.

We now live in a society in which the top few percent of Americans share little in common with everyone else. At the same time, they control all the levers of power over politics and the economy. Historically, this type of society does not endure for long. The facade might persist for a while, but as the system fails to respond to the needs of most people, especially during times of economic shocks, support for the system will erode. Eventually, the metaphorical dam breaks.

What will the next shock look like? What event will push the populace against the wall or through it? Will it be a government default, like the one that brought down Bourbon France? A financial crisis resulting from a disastrous foreign war, as happened to Russia in 1905? A crisis completely mishandled by a political establishment that is divorced from the daily life of workers, as occurred in Mexico in 1910? Maybe it will be some combination of all three, or something else. Whatever the cause, a broad range of possible futures becomes possible after a crisis. Some good, some bad, all a bit ugly. The long-term impacts may not be clear at the time.

We cannot predict with absolute certainty what might happen, but we think it is helpful to consider three possible scenarios: negative reconstruction, dystopian, and positive reconstruction. With these possible future scenarios in mind, we will look at how the kids and grandkids of our fictional 1980 high school graduates fare within each context. Our projections will only run through the 2060s.

The Negative Reconstruction Scenario

"At what point then is the approach of danger to be expected?" asked Abraham Lincoln in his Lyceum Address. "I answer, if it ever reaches us, it must spring up amongst us. It cannot come from abroad. If destruction be our lot, we must ourselves be its author and finisher. As a nation of freemen, we must live through all time or die by suicide."

When we use the term *reconstruction,* we mean that the political economy has fallen to pieces and must be put back together. This is the way that historians use the word to describe the period after the US Civil War, which had shattered the dominance of the rural aristocracy and ushered in the age of urban industrialists. The leadership class of the country was new, and the terms of the social contract were up in the air. A third of the country had been devastated by war, disease, and famine. In the other two-thirds of the country, people had to grapple with rapid industrialization and a broader definition of who could be a citizen. People at that time, understandably, saw a rapid escalation of labor militancy and the rise of the women's suffrage movement. Those efforts occurred while newly emancipated Black people tried to secure their place in the reconstruction South despite the vicious efforts of ex-Confederates to rebuild the Antebellum order.

Those conflicting movements—industrial versus rural, setting Black slaves free as others sought to limit their freedom—show us that post-crisis reconstruction efforts can be positive or negative. The new political economy after a major collapse can be worse than what existed before. When that happens, we (the authors) call it a *negative reconstruction.* The United States could experience a negative reconstruction. This might be a regional civil war against the government followed by the installation of incompetents. It could be violent revolution that installs a dictator, or a Yugoslav-style breakup of the country, or a "quiet" coup in which a demagogue gradually assumes dictatorial control. Whatever a negative reconstruction looks like, the country would take decades to recover. It might not recover at all.

Within the negative reconstruction scenarios, we think one is most likely: a Yugoslav-style breakup of the United States with a violent dissolution. We hope we are wrong, but there are a few reasons for our position. The US is geographically and culturally diverse. Multiple regions of the US operate economies large enough to put them each in the top ten GDPs in the world. The US faces no nearby military rivals that could use a moment of weakness to invade and topple the existing order. As Lincoln asked in the Lyceum address, "At what point shall we expect the approach of danger? By what means shall we fortify against it? Shall we expect some transatlantic military giant to step the Ocean and crush us at a blow? Never!"

So how might the US break up? We will assume that some near-term crisis pushes the federal government into collapse. Neither the military, the security state, nor citizens know how to save it. Regional leaders (e.g., governors, captains of industry) push for local autonomy or independence. The country splits into twelve parts, mainly so that each can have one of the twelve Federal Reserve headquarters as their respective central banks. That works fine for a while, but because there are opposing cultural and political values between the regions, they come into conflict with each other. Some regions with common values and economic interests team up against those with opposing values. All leaders and followers alike foolishly think conflict will be worth the cost. They believe that victory will come quickly and that they will all be home by Christmas.

The impacts of a violent national breakup would not occur evenly. We might imagine that most of the conflict occurs in the Mississippi and Ohio river valleys, between armed factions that coalesce around the Texas Triangle, the southern Appalachian Mountains, the Great Lakes, and the Northeast Corridor. The Pacific and Rocky Mountain regions, due to distance and degree of self-sufficiency, avoid the worst outcomes.

The economic impacts would also vary. Using Federal Reserve data for the GDPs of each of the twelve regions, we can estimate what each economy might look like during and after a conflict. To do this, we based our hypothetical scenario on the economic contractions caused by the Covid-19 recession. Because conflict can be so damaging to economies, we multiplied the Covid-19 contractions by twenty in the conflict's worst-hit areas. For the middle-hit areas, we multiplied the Covid-19 contraction by ten. For the least hit areas we multiplied the Covid-19 contraction by five. For each region, we compared the GDP forecast for 2027 with the GDP forecast for 2031, after a hypothetical conflict.

Without presenting all the granular math, we see that Federal Reserve District 1 (Boston) would see a 3.1 percent increase in GDP. Atlanta's district would see a GDP increase of 3.5 percent. Every other district would see a GDP decline. The worst decline would be the Cleveland district, with a 79.2 percent loss. St. Louis would see a decline of 53.9 percent. Richmond, Chicago, and Minneapolis would each experience a GDP decline of about 33 percent.

Even though Boston and Atlanta would have lackluster economic growth, the population in those regions could experience a decline in living standards. That is because refugees from hard-hit areas might move there to seek work. Jobs might be increasingly hard to find. Wages would decline as demand for goods and services slows. In other places in the Boston and Atlanta regions, unemployment might jump as factories and businesses lose access to markets and supply chains. One could expect to see an uptick in violent crime.

The middle-hit areas, except for New York, would see economic contractions of between 12 and 17 percent. Each year during the conflict, these regions would see a 4 to 6 percent loss of GDP. The most recent economic contraction of this sort happened from late 2008 through 2009 in the wake of the financial crisis. Imagine your local economy going through the Great Recession for the better part of three years. Estimates put the total number of business closures caused by the Great Recession at 1.8 million nationwide. Some thirty million people lost their jobs, and the official unemployment rate hit 10 percent. These numbers could have been much higher and the crisis would have lasted much longer if the federal government had not provided major support; specifically, trillions of dollars to keep the financial system afloat, and to bail out commercial banks and the big three Detroit automakers. In the event of a national breakup, such bailouts and stimulus spending would be unlikely because no one would want to buy debt from brand new quasi-countries engaged in active hostilities with their neighbors.

A national breakup would also disrupt supply chains more than the disruptions caused by the Covid-19 pandemic. Utilities would find it hard to keep the lights on using only local sources, resulting in rolling blackouts, temporarily hampering water and sewer services. Essential local functions like police, fire departments, and courts would see serious disruptions. One of the authors worked as an EMT during the Great Recession. The private ambulance service that provided 911 coverage for the city had to sell its contract to St. Francis Hospital due to financial problems. At one point in late 2009, the ambulance service's staff would race each other to cash paychecks before the payroll account ran out of money. Our partner agency, the Wilmington Fire Department, had to shutter one of its six stations every day for more than a year due to budget constraints, and it had to fire the lowest ranked firefighters on the seniority list. This increased emergency response times for citizens and cut into the wages of the firefighters themselves. Imagine what impacts might occur if such a situation continued for multiple years.

In our hypothetical scenario, the three worst-hit regions can be divided into two groups. The first group experiences losses of more than 30 percent, or about 1.1 percent each year. The economic impacts would be comparable to what occurred during the Great Depression of the 1930s. In that crisis, official unemployment reached 25 percent and whole groups of people traveled across the country looking for work. In Oklahoma, about 410,000 people out of a population of 2.4 million fled the state, mostly moving to California. Wages fell by about 60 percent. People who had money often could not find a place to spend it or save it because about nine thousand banks and eighty-six thousand businesses failed, effectively freezing local economies.

These impacts alone would be hard to cope with, but if the economic impacts went on for an extended time, the hardest-hit regions would see serious disruptions to basic infrastructure.

Maintaining public utilities would prove impossible, because large pumps and electrical transformers are made from nonlocal components. Those lucky enough to keep their homes would shiver through the winters and swelter during summer. Open-air sewers and complete power grid failures would become the norm. Medical facilities might become overwhelmed by disease outbreaks or shut down due to shortages of staff, equipment, and money.

The second group suffers a GDP contraction of between 50 and 80 percent. The impact would be, to put it mildly, catastrophic to human life. It might look like the impact of Hurricane Katrina on New Orleans. That storm killed at least twelve hundred people, drove 1.5 million from their homes, flooded 80 percent of the city, and caused $200 billion in infrastructure damage. A year after the storm, employment was 40 percent lower than in July 2005. The city lost about 50 percent of its population between 2005 and 2006, and it took about five years to regain 20 percent of the losses. This devastation would have been much worse had it not been for $60 billion in federal aid.

The impacts might also look like the human disaster caused by the Russian Civil War. That nation lost 10 percent of its prewar population due to violence and famine. The Volga and Don River basins suffered even more, losing about 30 percent of their prewar populations. Per-capita GDP, as measured in 1990 dollars, dropped from just under $1600 in 1913 to $600 in 1921. It only recovered to pre-revolution levels by 1930.[54]

With the devastation of Katrina and the Russian Civil War as guides, we can imagine that our hypothetical scenario would include a population decline of at least 50 percent. Emigration would account for most of this loss as people flee the Ohio and

Mississippi River valleys to regions of perceived safety. Imagine a third of your local friends, family, and neighbors leaving and never coming back. Those who stay with you are at the mercy of three apocalyptic horsemen: war, disease, and famine. Another third of your local friends, family, and neighbors contract illnesses and/or disabilities. Imagine the distended bellies of Americans standing in line for hours while hoping to receive sacks of flour delivered by UN peacekeepers, or imagine them being killed in an ambush while manning a 50-caliber machine gun welded to the cab of a jacked-up pickup.

The Children and Grandchildren of Jenny and Marty

We can speculate how Marty's three kids and Jenny's granddaughter might fare in a fragmented country formerly called the United States. They live in two of the hardest-hit regions, trying to survive as millions suffer grinding poverty and homelessness. Eight-two million people work hourly wage jobs. To force economic issues onto lawmakers' agendas, labor unions and non-unionized workers start a general strike in early 2028. The strikes slow the economy to a halt. However, instead of driving the bosses to the negotiating table, the nation's oligarchs double down on confrontation. The strike escalates over the spring and summer. The government attempts to bring the parties to the negotiating table. The workers do not trust the government and the oligarchs think they can force the issue in their favor, in part by hiring private mercenary groups to violently disperse the strikers. The violence in the streets backfires as the government loses control. Militias, paramilitaries, and law enforcement agencies seize control.

Marty's oldest son, Junior, works as a programmer and troubleshooter for a Michigan drone survey company at the outbreak of hostilities. Fearing for the safety of his wife and newborn child, he agrees to put his skills to work for a paramilitary group supported by the regional government, directing drone strikes against enemy combatants. To maintain some social status and better food and shelter for his family, Junior continues directing drone strikes against local rivals during the 2030s. By the 2040s, he and a half dozen other men rule Michigan as a *de facto* military junta, fronted by the facade of the old state government.

Marty's daughter, Jillian, always the overachiever, earned a scholarship to attend a Canadian medical school. As hostilities worsen, she and her husband run a minor emergency clinic in a small town near Lake Erie. As the fighting in Ohio escalates, paramilitaries execute a dozen patients and Jillian's husband after accusing him of giving aid to their enemies. Jillian escapes with their child across Lake Erie, spending several years in a refugee camp outside Toronto. Jillian uses her medical skills to care for sick people in exchange for extra food rations. Life in the camp is precarious. A cholera outbreak in 2035 almost claims both their lives. Citing the need for medical professionals, the Canadian government lets Jillian and her daughter out of the camp in 2037. They eventually settle in Quebec and never even talk about returning to the former US.

Little brother Bobby, unemployed in 2028, joins the picket lines early in the general strike. Embittered against the health care system and the profiteers who run it, which he believes caused his father's death, Bobby quickly takes a leadership role in a proworker organization called Strike Defenders. As violence escalates, the organization expands its efforts. In addition to protecting strikers' camps in public parks, the organization adopts combat tactics in central Ohio. Bobby rises to a prominent position as the right-hand man of the organization's militant leader. With the 2031 ceasefire, Bobby works feverishly to secure more weapons and fighters for an attack on what had been Michigan. Before the attack gets underway, a drone strike hits the staging area. Bobby becomes a double amputee. The lack of medical supplies and facilities leave Bobby with lingering health issues. He scrapes by with help from the organization's charitable operations for many years until he dies an early death in 2047.

In the winter of 2020, Jenny's car made it to Memphis before breaking down. Her granddaughter, Allison, spends her teens and early twenties hopping from job to job, trying to make money for the family. She sympathizes with the strikers, but Allison cannot afford to miss time at her minimum wage job. The first two years of violence did not affect the city too much, but now strikers launch an insurrection that seizes control of the city government and the transportation routes through and around Memphis. This move attracts the ire of the Tennessee governor's paramilitaries. Memphis endures a two hundred day siege before being overrun. The governor's forces sack the city and commit numerous atrocities and war crimes. Allison dies from malnutrition and disease just a few weeks after the announcement of the 2031 ceasefire.

Negative Reconstruction in 2060

History never ends, but for the purposes of this scenario, we will stop the timeline in the early 2060s, a century after Jenny, Marty, and Chad were born. Each region, depending on the severity of the economic impacts caused by the War of Dissolution, experiences different outcomes by 2060. The least-hit regions see an economic recovery by 2040, rebounding to pre-2028 levels. The citizens of these regions experience a return to relative normalcy from 2040 to 2060, but many of the economic and political elites from before the War remain in control, for better or worse. The middle-hit areas experience decades of economic stagnation, but by 2060 there are small signs of economic revival. The worst-hit regions suffer through years of fighting. Crop failures and epidemic disease follow swiftly in the wake of the fighting. The region's farmland, which had been the best in the world, is overgrown by invasive and opportunistic species. The area's population collapses to levels not seen since the 1920s. By the 2060s, the situation stabilizes, bringing the region back to a level of economic activity similar to the late 1970s, but most infrastructure is in ruins.

Overall, negative reconstruction results in new ruling groups cementing themselves in power. Each faction reacts to the War of Dissolution in unique ways. Some enact stopgap measures designed to address the inequalities that led to the breakup of the US in the first place. Others further entrench the power of the oligarchs. A third group pursues genuine, bottom-up reforms that represent a true break with the pre-dissolution world. Everyone has suffered a tremendous cost in lives and wealth.

The Dystopian Scenario

"No day ever dawns for the slave, nor is it looked for. For the slave it is all night—all night forever." Those words were written by the Reverend Germain W. Loguen in his book *As a Slave and As a Freeman: A Narrative of Real Life.* We quote Reverend Loguen not to conflate the conditions of modern Americans with that of chattel slaves in the Antebellum South. Rather, we think the quote is a metaphor for the current economic conditions of most Americans. Working people are enslaved by debt, high prices, and the lack of economic agency. How can people pursue other freedoms when they must perpetually scrape and scrounge for every penny, never able to create any store of wealth?

In the dystopian scenario, the United States does not fragment into conflicting regions. Rather, the dystopian condition emerges when policies and trends essentially continue unchanged. The oligarchs who control the political and economic establishment sideline or quash any movement that presents alternatives. This aggressive crushing of dissent fuels a low-level insurgency that challenges state power but never quite succeeds in replacing it. Meanwhile, the population faces impoverishment, declining lifespans, and narrowing options for economic betterment. This hypothetical scenario, which is quite different than the negative reconstruction scenario, could play out for two generations.

Within the broad dystopian category, outcomes after forty years could include widespread economic and social malaise, violence, and organized crime. We will consider three cases and what their impacts would be on a future United States dominated by oligarchs and a pliant federal government.

A real-world example of this scenario can be found in the decline of Argentina. In 1900, Argentina was one of the wealthiest economies in the world. A century later, the country's economy was in shambles. Over the course of the twentieth century, Argentinians suffered through a series of dictatorships and strongmen. Now its economic conditions are worse than the decades before World War I. In 1913, Argentina's annual per-capita GDP was $3,800 (in 1992 dollars). This compared favorably to France ($3,400) and Germany ($3,100). By 1992, Argentina's per-capita GDP had increased by about 80 percent to $6,800; however, that number had fallen far behind the per-capita GDP in France ($23,800) and Germany ($26,400). Long-term economic decline in Argentina fueled the rise of demagogues and authoritarian regimes, even if it never quite slipped into large-scale violent conflict.

What if Argentina's experience were to happen in the US? If we use 1980 as our starting point and 2060 as our ending point, and if we use the same 80 percent rise in GDP that Argentina saw, the US would see per-capita GDP go from $12,500 in 1980 to $22,500 in 2060. Compare that number to the current per-capita GDP in the US: $76,000. The United States of Dystopia would see a relative drop in per-capita GDP of more than $53,000.

A long-term economic decline would likely provoke an increase in violent crime. This often occurs in declining economies either because criminal organizations can exploit a weakening state (as in the case of Brazil) or because some violent groups are driven by destructive ideologies. An example of the former is the Mexican war against the cartels. An example of the second is the Shining Path insurgency in Peru.

Consider first the case of Peru in the 1990s. The communist Shining Path resistance movement used the impoverished Andean highlands and slums of Peru's cities as bases of operation for a decades-long insurgency against economic elites. The elites eventually defeated the Shining Path by applying copious state violence, but also by securing property rights for the poor and by improving engagement in the legal economy.[55]

Estimates of violence and crime are notoriously hard to estimate, but between roughly 1980 to 2000, the violence associated with the Shining Path insurgency killed about seventy thousand Peruvians. By comparison, the FBI recorded 21,570 homicides in the US in 2020. Remember that Peru's population was about twenty-five million people compared to the US population of more than three hundred million people.

As a response to the recruitment of unhoused, poor migrants in Peru's cities, famed economist Hernando de Soto Polar argued that a program of distributing property rights would incentivize potential gang members (or gang helpers) to stay in the "formal" economic system, because they would have property to defend. His idea exposed something macabre. It showed that the government had marginalized a large population by not giving them legal ability to purchase land. The fact that de Soto Polar's idea was necessary suggests a horrifying existence of undocumented Peruvians, a situation that is characteristic of failed nations. When people do not exist on paper, they have no government protections. They cannot open bank accounts. It should not be surprising that many Peruvians sought protection from the Shining Path. In a dystopian scenario, large populations can be pushed so far to the margins that they prefer the protection of a violent gang more than a constitutional government that fails to provide basic legal services and economic opportunities. Economic inequality can lead to insurgencies and political violence that never reaches the level of a full-blown revolution. Criminal gangs can fill the void created by a weak state and impoverished communities.

A sad current example is Haiti. Mexico is in much better condition than Haiti, but the country is struggling to counter the drug trade and human trafficking. Mexico's cartels have been fighting a low-grade civil war with the Mexican federal government since 2006. Estimates vary, but from 2006 to 2018 approximately 128,000 people have died because of drug gang violence. Since 2018, the death toll has only risen. This says nothing about potential spikes in deaths of despair from drug use or suicide. By some estimates, the violence reduced Mexico's annual economic growth by 1 percent over the last twenty years. These official numbers do not capture those who have fallen out of the official economy due to a lack of documentation or formal employment. As we have said, no matter how bad we think inequality is, it is worse.

Jenny, Marty, and Their Children and Grandchildren

Based on the histories of Mexico and Peru, we can imagine what might happen in a dystopian US economy. Economic despair and naked government-corporate collusion drives people to partake in a general strike in 2028. The conflict does not lead to armed conflict between organized groups, nor does it fracture the country into regional mini governments. Rather, the oligarchs rely on government force to undermine strikes. An out-of-control spiral of violence does not occur, but fringe ideological groups and organized crime networks increase levels of violence and intimidation. By 2048, twenty years after the national strike, the government and its corporate backers belatedly recognize the futility of their fight and, as in Peru, switch tactics. They pass "the Settlement" policy in 2050, which grants former insurgents amnesty, and they reduce legal barriers to self-employment. The reforms prove unpopular with the elites, who organize a coup in 2058.

Marty's oldest son, Junior, ends up working for the surveillance state. Artificial intelligence has supplanted many programmers and white collar workers, but it cannot substitute for loyal people who monitor those at odds with the state. The job security that comes with watching fringe ideological groups provides him with a stable income, even as those around him continue to struggle in economic desperation. Junior starts a family. He and his wife raise two children. However, as he ages toward retirement, Junior becomes increasingly bitter about the Settlement. When given the chance, he participates in the 2058 countercoup that puts pro-corporate hardliners back in charge of the federal government. This triggers a new insurgency in the early 2060s, which leads to continued rounds of terror campaigns against supporters of the state and endless government reprisals.

Marty's daughter, Jillian, finishes a medical degree in Canada and seriously considers leaving the US to avoid the ruinous debt payments she incurred to complete college and medical school. She marries and starts a family, but her clinic can never quite pay the bills. Her husband, injured during a protest in 2028, begins stealing meds from the clinic pharmacy and dies of an overdose in the 2037. The state of Ohio closes its clinic, citing unsafe storage of controlled substances. The real reason was that Jill would not pay a bribe to the state investigator. Debt strikes in the late 2030s lead to waves of economic terrorism and government reprisals. In 2038, a truck bombing at a payday loan office kills one of her kids. Crippling grief and depression follow. Jillian dies an anonymous death in a slum outside Cleveland in late 2050s, survived by an orphaned son who joins the underground insurgency forming in the wake of the 2058 coup.

Marty's youngest son, Bobby, who is unemployed at the time of the 2028 general strike, participates in the uprisings. With the failure of the strike, in 2031, the oligarchs and the government agree to use military action to take control of Venezuela's extensive oil fields, in part to distract the country from its ongoing internal conflicts. The government initiates a military draft, first by scooping up participants in the 2028 strike. Bobby flees the US for Mexico, where he finds work in the industrial north and lives as a semi-legal refugee. Like so many refugees throughout history, Bobby falls in love with a local. They marry and have a kid. Bobby takes advantage of a general amnesty for undocumented immigrants in 2049 and becomes a Mexican citizen. He misses his siblings, but Bobby never regrets the decision to cross the border.

Jenny's granddaughter, Allison, participates in the 2028 general strike. After the strike's failure, she and three coworkers form the Memphis Debt Collectors, a resistance movement that seeks to wipe out the debts of the poor, often by intimidating predatory creditors. When federal agents break up the group with surprise raids in 2036, Allison gets caught in the snare. She spends fourteen years in prison until she is released under the Settlement policy, but she must go into hiding after the 2058 coup. She hides in the flooded ruins of New Orleans, caught in a poverty trap with no health care. Allison dies of a tropical disease in 2060 at the age of forty-nine. After her death, the Memphis Debt Collectors become the subject of popular retellings and tall tales. They are portrayed as twenty-first century Robin Hoods, sources of heroic inspiration during what seems like a looming dark age.

The Dystopian Scenario in 2060

The dystopian scenario may be the least hopeful of the three possibilities. Since 2000, the US economy averaged 2 percent annual growth. If this growth rate continued from 2025 to 2060, the size of the economy would double to $57.4 trillion. The dystopian situation would undermine that positive outcome.

Once the oligarchs cement their political power in the wake of the hypothetical 2028 general strike, the trend toward greater inequality accelerates. Housing prices remain high, as does every form of debt. The interest paid by debtors will go to an ever-shrinking circle of massive banking conglomerates. Average wages decline, while profits continue to flow upward. Violence and crime further reduce economic growth, by as much as 1 percent per year. The economy could contract year over year, dropping from a peak of $30 trillion in 2030 to about $24 trillion in 2060.

Just as the economy stagnates and declines, so does the country's population. With more people choosing to have fewer children, due in part to economic costs, the native-born population ages. By 2050, the US population is seriously in decline. Ongoing domestic insurgency and crime, combined with diminishing work opportunities, make the dystopian United States much less appealing to immigrants. Without these new neighbors and their families, the US population hovers at 310 million rather than reaching the Census Bureau-projections of 404 million by 2060. Based on the Mexican and Peruvian models, US cemeteries would be populated with between 320,000 and 812,000 Americans in unmarked graves during the 2030s and 2040s. Many of those poor souls would be twentysomething victims of insurgent violence. With the demographic loss of people in their prime economic and childbearing ages, the economic effects might be far reaching. As the US grapples with a domestic insurgency and economic decline, the rest of the world would be less interested in trading partnerships. Those countries might decide to shift away from the dollar as their reserve currency, which would compound the self-inflicted economic damage.

By the 2060s, the US economy would be 10 to 16 percent smaller than today's. A new round of insurgency might not be driven by people seeking to create a better economic order; rather, they might be driven by nihilist rage, or religious fervor, or any other idea that captures the collective imagination of debt-bound people who are treated as disposable human beings by their social superiors. Making projections beyond the next two generations is difficult, but the dystopian scenario might resemble the latter years of the Soviet Union: the oligarchy's government shambling from one crisis to another, never quite dying, but never experiencing a true renaissance.

The Positive Reconstruction Scenario

American novelist Jack London wrote: "A bone to the dog is not charity. Charity is the bone shared with the dog when you are just as hungry as the dog."[56] London grew up poor in late nineteenth-century California. He experienced the cruelties of an oligarchic system. Underlying the quote above is the question of how average Americans can afford to help our fellow citizens when we can barely help ourselves? And how can we change the trajectory of the US economy when we lack power and influence?

We can all hope that a positive reconstruction scenario becomes reality. In this case, a mass movement emerges that successfully challenges the economic and political power of the oligarchs without causing a constitutional crisis or a national breakup. We do not think that political leaders of either party will bring about that type of change; rather, change will require a grassroots movement led by people who know the cost and value of true charity.

And how might true, positive reconstruction come about? This change could occur in several ways. For example, a couple of compassionate oligarchs might recognize the precarity of our situation, break ranks with their fellow billionaires, and cross the metaphorical picket line. This has happened before in American history. Presidents Theodore and Franklin Roosevelt both recognized the needs of common people and acted against their own class interests to push meaningful reforms. Theodore Roosevelt broke up monopolies and added workplace protections that helped millions of Progressive Era Americans. In 1933, Franklin Roosevelt entered office at a time when it looked like the project of liberal democracy and free-market capitalism had failed. The New Deal offered not only economic and material assistance to US citizens; it represented a viable response to the rising tide of fascism and communism. The New Deal gave people some hope by establishing programs like Social Security, rural electrification, and the Works Progress Administration. Today, however, hoping for a self-aware billionaire or political leader to save us seems foolish, to put it mildly.

There is another route to real reform: the emergence of a movement based on class solidarity between the poor, working, and middle classes. The movement could put significant pressure on the top income brackets to finally recognize that the economy runs only because the lower and middle classes show up to work. Perhaps a general strike would push lawmakers to enact specific reforms, to steer the ship of state away from the metaphorical iceberg. Those reforms could open the door for new political leaders who have never made six figures and who are not beholden to billionaires. By 2040, a new consensus takes hold that only those representing the working majority belong in state and national governments.

Yet another route to a positive reconstruction scenario occurs when people recognize their collective power as consumers. They disinvest themselves from the current economic model. In addition to founding co-ops and mutual aid societies, they refuse to buy products from companies owned by oligarchs. In this scenario, enough working people withhold financial and labor support from massive businesses to cause the breakup or collapse of America's largest corporations, thereby reducing their political influence. This route would enrich the rest of us and breathe new life into local economies. This third approach to reform is highly appealing because it requires no wrangling with a corrupt political establishment. It only requires that consumers (collectively) defund the oligarchs.

In the positive reconstruction scenario, *democracy* is not merely a buzzword. Rather, citizens participate in the change, both at work and in the community. It would lead to a truly free market. A diverse array of firms would compete at the local and regional levels to efficiently provide the best goods and services, and the surplus wealth generated by those firms would stay with the employees of those companies. The profits would not be siphoned off by distant financial institutions and shareholders. Ideally, Americans would see their wealth grow in alignment with the nation's GDP, as occurred in the 1950s and 1960s, and experience a rebirth of cultural and civic spirit.

And what might such a new economic order look like? What sorts of incomes would Americans enjoy if they owned the companies they worked for? What if the tax code did not give massive support to the rich?

At the beginning of the book, we presented the RAND Corporation's findings that approximately $50 trillion had *trickled up* to the wealthiest sectors of the economy during the previous forty years. Using that study as a basis, we can ask what incomes might have looked like if that redistribution of wealth to top income brackets had not occurred. When we do the math, we discover that income goes up for everyone except for those in the top 1 percent. Even an income earner in the top 5 percent would see a small jump in income. So, there should be plenty of widespread, diversified support for a positive reconstruction effort.

	Current (2025)	2065 Current Trends	2065 Positive Reconstruction
25th %	$39,600	$46,728	$85,932
Median	$62,000	$73,160	$134,540
75th %	$97,200	$136,080	$210,924
90th %	$159,600	$274,512	$347,928
95th %	$229,200	$479,028	$498,510
99th %	$949,200	$2,809,632	$697,662
Top 1 % Mean	$1,660,800	$7,938,624	$755,664

Figure 10-1: Comparison of incomes in a status quo economy versus a positive reconstruction scenario, 2025 and 2065.

Looking at figure 10-1, we can see that if current policies persist, Americans earning a median income would take home $61,000 less in wages in 2065 than they would if Americans could sustain a positive reconstruction scenario (using the RAND study as a baseline). Such a movement, let us call it American Solidarity, would not be easy, but with widespread unity, it could successfully browbeat both political parties into embracing thorough economic reforms without moving the nation toward communism. Again, the goal is to create *rules* that work equally for all people—not just the top 1 percent—within a healthy free market system.

We say both political parties for a reason. Pushing the oligarch-backed candidates out of *both parties* would prevent our elections from turning into a red versus blue, urban versus rural referendum that divides us as Americans. Additionally, in the American electoral system, third parties operate at a perpetual disadvantage, so their candidates are extremely unlikely to muster enough support to replace one of the two oligarch-controlled parties.

Is such a strategy workable? Could people of all economic classes on both sides of the proverbial aisle work together for a shared goal? Fortunately, history is not only full of negative examples. In the 1960s, environmentalism found considerable support in both parties. A Democrat-controlled Congress passed the Clean Air Act, the Clean Water Act, and created the Environmental Protection Agency. Republican President Richard Nixon, of all people, signed those bills into law with the support of environmentalists within his own party. So, despite the obstacles, we think it is possible to convince voters in both political parties to vote out corporate-sponsored legislators at the state and federal levels, and to forge a clear set of demands for economic reform. Collective strength is essential. That could start by organizing ourselves into civic groups that meet at least three criteria: open to political discourse; large enough to reach a critical mass of potential voters; and operate outside the direct control of oligarchs. An initial list of organizations that meet these criteria include labor unions and some churches. Both groups have, in the past, openly supported movements that sought to change the US economic order.

To be clear, an American Solidarity movement should not control these organizations because they would quickly become targets for state harassment or even violence. Rather, American Solidarity should use the organizations as venues for people to discuss and implement ways to produce systemic change.

Oklahoma, the authors' home state, provides a great example. In its initial decades of statehood, Oklahoma churches often hosted revivals during which speakers called openly for attendees to vote for candidates who would overturn the economic order. Like churches today, rural parishes tiptoed right up to the line of political speech without stepping over it. In the 1910s and 1920s, Oklahoma's impoverished sharecroppers saw the Socialist Party as the only one that would hold wealthy landowners to account for stolen wages, evictions, and other abuses. At one point, Oklahoma City elected a socialist mayor. Numerous local offices were occupied by members of the Socialist Party. It is no coincidence that the first Oklahoma state flag had a solid red background with a large white star in the middle. After the Red Scare of the early 1920s, the state legislature retired the maybe-a-bit-too-left-leaning red flag and created the current flag with its light blue background and an Osage war shield.

This anecdote from Oklahoma's past shows that Americans, even in red states, have a long tradition of fighting the oligarchic economic order. Look at your local history. Find ideas about how communities previously organized against exploitation and abuse. We suspect that your state has a rich tradition of "sticking it to the man." Did every effort succeed? No. Oklahoma in 2024 is hardly a hotbed of anti-establishment thinking. Nevertheless, real change is possible.

Jenny, Marty, Their Children and Grandchildren

How might a positive reconstruction scenario affect our fictional characters' children and grandchildren? As with the previous scenarios, the grinding impoverishment of those outside elite circles drives labor unions and non-unionized workers to start a general strike in early 2028. Groups of concerned citizens within unions and churches call on people who work in certain sectors to call in sick and take a day to "walk in the park."

Due to widespread nonpartisan participation, the strikes are surprisingly successful. The economy grinds to a halt. Ports close. Truckers stop driving. Teachers do not show up for class. Stores close. Corporate offices are empty. However, America's oligarchs double down on confrontation by relying on government force. Because the strikers and protesters are peaceful, that tactic backfires. Fence-sitters begin to sympathize with the movement. Those not actively participating in the strikes refuse to pay taxes or patronize corporations run by oligarchs, or those who oppose American Solidarity. During the next election, people vote to remove state and federal politicians who support the oligarchy. Many people leave their employment with big firms in favor of starting, or joining, existing cooperatives and employee-owned firms.

Marty's oldest son, Junior, who has a degree in cybersecurity, ends up working in corporate security for a firm that supports the status quo. He thinks the American Solidarity movement is filled with dupes and wild-eyed anarchists. After the general strike and the great conglomerate breakups of the early 2030s, Junior moves his wife and kids abroad. They first travel to Europe and then to the Russian Federation where Junior works for a St. Petersburg-based cybersecurity firm. The family settles in a neighborhood dominated by American immigrants who left the US to follow their oligarch bosses. After many bitter years resenting the new order, Junior finally invites his brother and sister to a family reunion at a *dacha* outside St. Petersburg in 2053.

Jillian, with her medical degree, returns to the US from Canada just as the general strike heats up. She and her husband spend free time providing first aid and emergency surgeries to people in need. Congress, in the wake of the general strike, passes a cornerstone law that breaks up medical insurance monopolies and bans private equity firms from owning hospital networks. Jillian, her husband, and their clinic's medical staff restructure their clinic, operating it as a worker-owned co-op. Jillian lives a quiet life with a clear conscience, a good salary, and a stable marriage with three kids.

Marty's youngest son, Bobby, participates in the general strike and quickly joins the militant side of his local American Solidarity organization. Deeply angered by violent police actions against protesters in a local park, he comes within hours of driving a truck full of explosives to a police station in downtown Detroit. Word reaches him, just in time, that the governor resigned and appointed a labor leader as the replacement, effectively giving in to the protestors' demands. After several years, and seeing that reforms are working, Bobby ends up working for a reformed police department that focuses on policing violent crime rather than on criminalizing poverty and vice. By the end of the 2050s, he retires as a captain and moves to northern Ohio to be closer to Jillian and his nieces and nephews.

Jenny's granddaughter, Allison, joins Solidarity Memphis. She gathers intel and plans demonstrations. She never opts for the violent side of the movement, but she is nevertheless arrested on trumped-up charges and spends several years in jail. With the election of a pro-Solidarity governor, she and many others are released in 2033. A year later, Memphis voters elect her as a state representative. Her experience with the movement makes her an ideal legislator to oversee the implementation of Tennessee's revocation of corporate charters, and the turning over of corporate assets to employees.

Allison eventually leaves public office, deciding to run a repurposed strip mall that is home to for-profit businesses and mutual aid organizations. The economy is much more equitable, but people still have problems that require a helping hand. On this path forward, Allison enjoys a quiet home life with her wife, adopting a pair of orphans whose single mother died in the protests.

The Positive Reconstruction Scenario in 2060

No scenario, even this optimistic one, can run its course free of violence. It is important to remember that Poland's communist government tried to suppress that nation's solidarity movement in the 1980s. At least one hundred people died during strikes and protests. About fifteen thousand people were arrested. Many more lost their jobs. As many as seven hundred thousand people left Poland in the years between the declaration of martial law and the end of the communist government in 1989.

Post-communist Poland experienced a short-term economic contraction from 1989 to 1992. This was followed by a few years of moderate growth through 1994 and then robust growth through 1999. The World Bank estimates that the Polish economy was 20 percent larger in 1999 than it was in 1989.

It would not be surprising to see similar events unfold during and after an American Solidarity movement and a positive reconstruction effort. In the US, the solidarity effort would likely be met with resistance. The oligarchy will find it unthinkable to relinquish power, money, and influence to average people. The US has a much larger population than Poland, so the movement could lead to a higher number of deaths, injuries, and emigrations between the time of the general strike in 2028 and 2033.

However, just as Poland experienced long-term economic growth, we would expect the US economy to also rebound after a temporary contraction. We doubt that the US economy would grow by 20 percent in a decade, as was the case in Poland; nevertheless, the US would grow considerably in a post-reform era. Newly approved economic policies designed to prevent the redistribution of wealth to the top 1 percent would enable average Americans to gain an additional $15 trillion for their hard work. This would occur, in part, by giving ownership of publicly listed companies to the employees, as described earlier. Profit sharing plans in smaller firms would spark wage increases and economic growth, because a huge population of average Americans would have more to spend.

Epilogue

The scenarios described in the previous chapter represent only three of the myriad possibilities before us. The future will probably include a mix of scenarios, with one being more dominant while incorporating flavors of the other two. Perhaps the coming decades will see a peaceful dissolution of the country. Or perhaps the dystopian economic order will persist unchanged. Perhaps the government will approve a few policy reforms to stave off decades of terrorism. Or maybe a positive reconstruction will be met with more resistance from the oligarchs than imagined. Perhaps an American Solidarity movement will win out, but only after an economic depression that galvanizes popular action.

Additionally, these scenarios do not account for an unlimited array of external tragedies, disruptions, and shocks. The US could face climate change impacts sooner and more severely than imagined. The long-term effects of artificial intelligence could be nothing more than an amusing flash-in-the-pan, or the technology could lead to widespread layoffs. We can only speculate how the rest of the world might react to American weakness, whether prolonged or temporary. Even if a positive reconstruction scenario occurs, other governments might see the collapse of corporate America as an opportunity to seize US assets abroad. Or would they provide safe havens for the billions of dollars held by US oligarchs who would likely move money (and themselves) abroad to avoid interactions with American "peasants."

Maybe the future course of the United States will weave back and forth, first on the dystopian path, then perhaps veering into the danger zones of negative reconstruction. Perhaps the violence and turmoil will startle people enough to turn them toward the more hopeful path of positive reconstruction. Much of America's collective journey involves stumbling from one path to the other. History happens unevenly and sometimes without rhyme or reason. As Israeli diplomat Abba Eban stated back in 1967, "Men and nations behave wisely when they have exhausted all other resources."[57] The authors hope that we will not wait to exhaust all other alternatives before we choose to do the right thing.

Academic research about economic inequality has languished over the last forty years or so, but it is belatedly making a comeback. Thomas Pikkety published a popularization of his research in *Capital in the Twenty-First Century*. Nobel Prize-winners Daron Acemoglu and James Robinson, along with Simon Johnson, have contributed to the renewed interest in inequality through their discussion on extractive and inclusive economic institutions. They point out ways in which inequality can lead to the failure of macroeconomics and, by extension, nations. Interest in inequality has been present in the work of Debraj Ray and others. Nobel Prize-winning economist Sir Angus Deaton published his 2023 book about inequality titled *Economics in America*.

That this academic research about the subject is so overdue reflects the fact that US inequality is stealthy. The extreme stratification caused by economic inequality means that many Americans never spend meaningful time with anyone outside their own class. This masks the severity of economic inequality for those who do not experience its worst effects. We hope that the data, ideas, and narratives in this book expand our collective understanding about inequality and its dangers. We hope the book enables everyone to better navigate the treacherous waters in which we *all* find ourselves.

Stories have long been a way for people to make sense of the world, so let us leave you with a pair of narratives from none other than J. R. R. Tolkien. It may feel as though we are at Helm's Deep, playing the part of beleaguered last defenders of humanity, facing wave after wave of Orcs hellbent on snuffing out our families and communities. We look desperately to the East for the rising sun, for a charge of the Rohirrim, and a for Gandalf to save the day. But despair can lead a few people to acts of violence which, however temporarily satisfying, do not end the onslaught. Tolkien knew this and placed at the heart of his epic the battle within each of us.

Instead, Tolkien takes us to Mount Doom where we all struggle with the temptation of the One Ring. It would be easy to put on the ring, become invisible, and try to hide from an economic system that has become like the Dark Lord Sauron: cruel, malicious, hungry to dominate all life. But we cannot remain invisible forever. Sauron's agents will find us, and they will reclaim the ring. Therefore, we must choose the path that, however hard and painful, enables us to cast the ring into the fire. The ring is not destroyed by violence and force, but by casting it back into the fires that made it. In the end, the smallest, unlikeliest heroes save Middle Earth. Most of all, do not give in to fear and despair. Economic inequality resulted from human designs; therefore, it can be *redesigned* by us.

The preamble to the US Constitution begins this way: "We the people, in order to form a more perfect union . . ." That line was intentional. We are all in this together.

Acknowledgements

First and foremost, I want to acknowledge my loving wife. Without her understanding and support, this book would have remained little more than long text chains with my coauthor. I owe a great deal to my parents, friends, and teachers. Would that we all had the kind of people to whom I have looked for guidance and illumination, even when the skies darkened and the shadows grew long. "We can see so far because we stand on the shoulders of giants" (attributed to Isaac Newton).

Ben Johnson

I wish to thank Arely, first and foremost, for the guidance, counsel, support, and love. I am grateful for Fable and Elias, who always kept me honest. For my dear friend and coauthor Ben, who pushed forward when I struggled. For professor William A. Barnett, who always provided his wisdom and guidance. I wish to thank those who contributed through deep conversation and debate, including Dr. Paul Mattson, Elizabeth Wroe, Lynn and Pam Mattson, Antonio and Dina Briones, Dr. Leah Johnson, Brian Mattson, Dr. Brandli "Lee" Stitzel, Dr. Sasha Lugovskyy, and Dr. Travis Whitacre.

Dr. Ryan Mattson

Endnotes

1   Marion Laboure and Nicolas Deffrennes, *Democratizing Finance: The Radical Promise of Fintech,* Harvard University Press, 2022, p. 11.

2   Economic Policy Institute, "The Productivity-Pay Gap," May 15, 2025, https://www.epi.org/productivity-pay-gap/.

3   Carter C. Price and Kathryn A. Edwards, "Trends in Income From 1975 to 2018," RAND, September 14, 2020, https://www.rand.org/pubs/working_papers/WRA516-1.html.

4   United States Census Bureau, "Census Bureau Releases New 2020 Census Data on Age, Sex, Race, Hispanic Origin, Households and Housing," May 25, 2023, https://www.census.gov/newsroom/press-releases/2023/2020-census-demographic-profile-and-dhc.html.

5   United States Census Bureau, "Census Bureau Releases New 2020 Census Data."

6   Alexander Hermann, "8 Facts About Investor Activity in the Single-Family Rental Market," Joint Center for Housing Studies of Harvard University, July 18, 2023, https://www.jchs.harvard.edu/blog/8-facts-about-investor-activity-single-family-rental-market#:~:text=The%20number%20of%20single%2Dfamily%20rentals%20then%20fell%20in%20more,33%20percent%20of%20all%20renters.

7   Laurie Goodman, Jung Hyun Choi, and Jun Zhu, "The 'Real' Homeownership Gap between Today's Young Adults and Past Generations Is Much Larger Than You Think," Urban Institute, April 17, 2023, https://www.urban.org/urban-wire/real-homeownership-gap-between-todays-young-adults-and-past-generations-much-larger-you.

8   Federal Reserve Bank of St. Louis.

9   Federal Reserve Bank of St. Louis.

10   Heather Vogell, "Justice Department Sues Six of the Nation's Largest
        Landlords in Effort to Stop Alleged Price-Fixing in Rental Markets,"
        ProPublica, January 9, 2025, https://www.propublica.org/article/justice-
        department-sues-landlords-alleged-price-fixing-realpage-rent.

11   US Department of Justice, "Justice Department Sues RealPage for
        Algorithmic Pricing Scheme that Harms Millions of American Renters,"
        August 23, 2024, https://www.justice.gov/archives/opa/pr/justice-
        department-sues-realpage-algorithmic-pricing-scheme-harms-millions-
        american-renters.

12   David Prock, "What Led to the Abandonment of Vista Shadow Mountain
        Apartments In Tulsa?" News On 6, September 26, 2024, https://www.
        newson6.com/story/66f5928959b727c09e5a311e/timeline-what-led-to-
        the-abandonment-of-vista-shadow-mountain-apartments-in-tulsa#.

13   Martin Gilens, *Affluence and Influence: Economic Inequality and Political
        Power in America*, (Princeton University Press, 2012).

14   David Brooks, "The Nuclear Family Was a Mistake," *The Atlantic*, March
        2020, https://www.theatlantic.com/magazine/archive/2020/03/the-
        nuclear-family-was-a-mistake/605536/.

15   Foundation for Community Association Research (FCAR), "Community
        Association Fact Book 2021."

16   Ben Mace, "New Plan almost Doubles Homes in Proposed Smyrna
        Development," Delaware Online, January 15, 2021, https://www.
        delawareonline.com/story/news/2021/01/15/smyrna-approves-
        preliminary-plan-709-homes-near-sunnyside-elementary/6621940002/.

17   US Census Bureau count of housing units: 146 million units multiplied by
        the rental rate of 35 percent.

18   US Government Accounting Office, "F-35 Joint Strike Fighter:
        More Actions Needed to Explain Cost Growth and Support Engine
        Modernization Decision," May 30, 2023, https://www.gao.gov/products/
        gao-23-106047.

19   Raj Chetty et al., "The Fading American Dream: Trends in Absolute
        Income Mobility Since 1940," National Bureau of Economic Research,
        Working Paper 22910, 2017, https://www.nber.org/papers/w22910.

20   Frank Newport and Joy Wilke, "Desire for Children Still Norm in U.S.,"
      Gallup, September 25, 2013, https://news.gallup.com/poll/164618/desire-
      children-norm.aspx.

21   Kalea Hall, "GM to Increase Dividend 25%, Buy Back another $6
      Billion of Shares," Reuters, February 26, 2025, https://www.reuters.
      com/markets/deals/gm-increase-dividend-by-25-buy-back-another-6-
      billion-shares-2025-02-26/#:~:text=GM%20in%20June%202024%20
      approved,quarter%20earnings%20call%20last%20month.

22   General Motors, SEC Filings, https://investor.gm.com/sec-filings; Stock
      Dividend Screener (SDS), "A Peek into General Motors (GM) Share
      Buyback History," November 22, 2024, https://stockdividendscreener.
      com/auto-manufacturers/general-motors-stock-buyback-history/#share-
      buyback.

23   Allison Morrow and Chris Isidore, "GM Lavishes Shareholders with Cash
      Weeks after Saying it Couldn't Afford Workers' Demands," CNN Business,
      November 29, 2023, https://www.cnn.com/2023/11/29/business/gm-
      lavishes-shareholders-with-cash-weeks-after-stingy-wage-offer-for-workers.

24   Internal Revenue Service, "Individual Income Tax Returns Complete
      Report, 2021," accessed June 2025, https://www.irs.gov/pub/irs-prior/
      p1304--2024.pdf#page=24.

25   American Academy of Arts and Sciences, "Humanities' Share of All
      Advanced Degrees Conferred," 2021, https://www.amacad.org/humanities-
      indicators/higher-education/humanities-share-all-advanced-degrees-
      conferred.

26   Finance Authority of Maine, Student Loan/Salary Calculator, accessed
      June 2025, https://www.famemaine.com/affording-education/pay-for-
      school/resources-tools/calculators/student-loan-salary-calculator/.

27   Economic Policy Institute, "The Productivity-Pay Gap."

28   Daniel Calingaert, "Dismantle the Global Financial Secrecy System,"
      Global Financial Integrity, June 6, 2024, https://gfintegrity.org/dismantle-
      the-global-financial-secrecy-system/.

29   Alan Blinder, *A Monetary and Fiscal History of the United States, 1961-
      2021*, (Princeton University Press, 2022).

30   Orazio P. Attanasio and Luigi Pistaferri, "Consumption Inequality," *Journal of Economic Perspectives* 30, no. 2 (2016): 3–28, https://www.aeaweb.org/articles?id=10.1257/jep.30.2.3.

31   Orazio P. Attanasio and Luigi Pistaferri, "Consumption Inequality."

32   Daron Acemoglu and Simon Johnson, *Power and Progress: Our 1000-Year Struggle Over Technology and Prosperity*, (Public Affairs, 2023), p. 259.

33   Daron Acemoglu and Simon Johnson, *Power and Progress*, p. 17.

34   Ed Conway, *Material World: The Six Raw Materials that Shape Modern Civilization*, (Knopf, 2023).

35   David Brooks, "The Nuclear Family Was a Mistake."

36   US Department of Justice, Office of Public Affairs, "Department of Justice Prevails in Landmark Antitrust Case Against Google," April 17, 2025, https://www.justice.gov/opa/pr/department-justice-prevails-landmark-antitrust-case-against-google.

37   Bobby Allyn, "The Biggest Trial in Meta's History Starts Monday. Here's What to Know," NPR, April 13, 2025, https://www.npr.org/2025/04/13/nx-s1-5358434/ftc-meta-antitrust-trial.

38   GlobalData, "Apple's Number of Employees (FY2017 – FY2022)," accessed June 2025, https://www.globaldata.com/data-insights/technology-media-and-telecom/apples-Number-of-employees/.

39   US Securities and Exchange Commission, Annual Report for Apple, September 30, 2023, https://www.annualreports.com/HostedData/AnnualReportArchive/a/NASDAQ_AAPL_2023.pdf.

40   Tipalti, "Profit per Employee," accessed June 2025, https://tipalti.com/profit-per-employee/.

41   Drew DeSilver and Luona Lin, "Blue-Collar Workers Are Less Satisfied at Work, Less Attached to Their Jobs than Other U.S. Workers," Pew Research, March 31, 2025, https://www.pewresearch.org/short-reads/2025/03/31/blue-collar-workers-are-less-satisfied-at-work-less-attached-to-their-jobs-than-other-us-workers/.

42   Tom Polansek, "Stung by Pandemic and JBS Cyberattack, U.S. Ranchers Build New Beef Plants," Reuters, June 17, 2021, https://www.reuters.com/world/the-great-reboot/stung-by-pandemic-jbs-cyberattack-us-ranchers-build-new-beef-plants-2021-06-17/.

43   Jack Kelly, "Wells Fargo Forced to Pay $3 Billion for the Bank's Fake Account Scandal," Forbes, February 24, 2020, https://www.forbes.com/sites/jackkelly/2020/02/24/wells-fargo-forced-to-pay-3-billion-for-the-banks-fake-account-scandal/.

44   US Department of Justice, "Wells Fargo Agrees to Pay $3 Billion to Resolve Criminal and Civil Investigations into Sales Practices Involving the Opening of Millions of Accounts without Customer Authorization," February 21, 2020, https://www.justice.gov/archives/opa/pr/wells-fargo-agrees-pay-3-billion-resolve-criminal-and-civil-investigations-sales-practices.

45   Macrotrends, "Wells Fargo Net Income 2010-2025," Accessed June 2025, https://www.macrotrends.net/stocks/charts/WFC/wells-fargo/net-income.

46   Michael I. Norton and Dan Ariely, Building a Better America—One Wealth Quintile at a Time, *Perspectives on Psychological Science* 6, no. 1 (2011): 9–12, https://www.hbs.edu/ris/Publication%20Files/Norton_Michael_Building%20a%20better%20America%20One%20wealth%20quintile%20at%20a%20time_4c575dff-fe1d-4002-b61a-1227d08b71be.pdf.

47   David MCullough, *John Adams*, (Touchstone, 2001), p. 134.

48   Christian Morrison and Wayne Snyder, "The Income Inequality of France in Historical Perspective," *European Review of Economic History* 4, (2000): 59-83, http://piketty.pse.ens.fr/files/MorrissonSnyder2000.pdf.

49   Steven Nafziger and Peter H. Lindert, "Russian Inequality on the Eve of Revolution," National Bureau of Economic Research, Working Paper 18383, September 2012, https://www.nber.org/papers/w18383.

50   William Strauss and Neil Howe, *The Fourth Turning: What the Cycles of History Tell Us about America's Next Rendezvous with Destiny*, (Crown Publishing, 1997).

51 Jill Lepore, "The Failed Ideas That Drive Elon Musk," *The New York Times*, April 4, 2025, https://www.nytimes.com/2025/04/04/opinion/elon-musk-doge-technocracy.html?searchResultPosition=1.

52 Andrew Duehren, "Rich Gain and Poor Lose in Republican Policy Bill, Budget Office Finds," *The New York Times*, June 12, 2025, https://www.nytimes.com/2025/06/12/us/politics/rich-poor-republican-bill.html.

53 Andrew Duehren, "Rich Gain and Poor Lose in Republican Policy Bill,"

54 Mark Harrison and Andrei Markevich, "Russia's Home Front, 1914-1922: The Economy," Centre for Competitive Advantage in the Global Economy, Working Paper, 2012, https://warwick.ac.uk/fac/soc/economics/research/centres/cage/publications/workingpapers/2012/russias_home_front_1914_1922_the_economy/.

55 Hernando de Soto Polar's work on "The Other Path" and "The Mystery of Capital" attempts to explain these efforts. Their actual contributions relative to the state violence are debatable.

56 Jack London, "A Reminiscence and a Confession," *Cosmopolitan* 43, no.1 (1907): 17-22, https://archive.org/details/sim_cosmopolitan_1907-05_43_1/page/18/mode/2up.

57 Robert Trumbull, "Japan Welcomes Eban Warmly; Her Industry Impresses Israeli," *The New York Times*, March 19, 1967, https://www.nytimes.com/1967/03/19/archives/japan-welcomes-eban-warmly-her-industry-impresses-israeli.html?searchResultPosition=2.

Index